President
Droupadi Murmu
(Rairangpur to Raisina Hills)

Dr. Gopal Sharma

DIAMOND BOOKS

www.diamondbook.in

Publisher : **Diamond Pocket Books (P) Ltd.**
X-30, Okhla Industrial Area, Phase-II
New Delhi-110020
Phone : 011-40712100
E-mail : sales@dpb.in
Website : www.dpb.in
Edition : 2022

President Droupadi Murmu (Rairangpur to Raisina Hills)
By - *Dr. Gopal Sharma*

Publisher's Note..

Her Excellency President Droupadi Murmu Ma'am, Heartiest Congratulations to you on becoming the President of India.

You would be happy to know that Diamond Books has published the first ever book based on your life-- President Droupadi Murmu: Rairangpur to Raisina Hills. We are proud of this achievement. We had taken the decision to publish this book on the very day your name was announced. You possess an extraordinary personality.

I have learnt about your life from newspapers and Doordarshan programmes, and was very inspired by your formidable strength, forbearance, and dialectics. A tribal woman, who travelled from Rairangpur village to Bhuvaneshwar to attain education, is an example for all women. When you entered politics, you received the Neelkanth prize. This is a great learning for all those who wish to step into politics.

When you became the governor, your welfare policies and people friendly decisions made the common people to trust in your leadership, and this was a great achievement. You have risen out of every depression to involve yourself in social challenges. Your character is not one to accept failure, but to move forward with unrelenting self-confidence. Your becoming the President of India is a matter of pride for all of us. We believe that your life will be an inspiration to give us all courage to overcome struggles. In your first speech, you have made a significant statement that India is a country where if a girl from a village decides to move from the village to the city for her education, then she can overcome any hurdles, and it is not difficult for her to become an MLA, a minister, governor and even the highest consitutional post of the country—President of India.

It is due to the tireless efforts of the writer of this book, Mr. Gopal Sharma, that it has been possible to publish this book. We shall remain always grateful to him for this. We are publishing this book very soon into various Indian languages so that our countryman should have knowledge about you.

—Narender Kumar Verma

nk@dpb.in

Contents

Chapter One
The Nomination: An Epic Choice

I am extremely thrilled. It has been a part of our ideology. My late father, P.S. Sangma, had once said that a tribal person would someday become the President of India. It is a dream come true for all of us. We are supporting her candidature. India's 1st Indigenous Tribal Woman as our country's President. As President, Smt Droupadi Ji will represent a New India. She represents hope for every tribal, every girl, every woman, and will carry with her the aspirations of small communities of India. We are proud of her & wish her all the best for the upcoming Presidential Election.

—Meghalaya CM Conrad Sangma

"Making of the *pratham nagrik*"

When in June people perspire and wait for rain
An epic-choice was made
To bring the marginalised into the mainstream
In Times like these
A name was proposed
For the Presidentship of India
And within a month or so
History was made.

I narrate with ease the events that occurred within the last thirty days or so. I was busy jotting down everything I heard, saw and read when others were engaged in their mundane affairs. But I will not waste your time in telling you my story. You are here to read her story. So read on.

Presidents so far

This is the seventy fifth year of India's independence. On 26th January 2023, the new President, Mahamahim Droupadi Murmu, is going to address the nation in Hindi. She is the fifteenth President of the Republic of India. India has had fourteen presidents before her. All were men but one. India's previous presidents had been chosen from different walks of life. Many distinguished personalities and visionaries, including educationalists, diplomats, veteran Parliamentarians, scientists, and freedom fighters, adorned and embellished the office of the President. There are freedom fighters, a comparative religions' scholar, a trade unionist, a missile scientist, a retired bureaucrat and accomplished diplomat, an academician, and a multitude of politicians in the resplendent galaxy of the presidents of the Indian Republic. All other major groups, such as Muslims, Dalits, Sikhs, and women— have been represented except the tribal community or other backward classes (OBCs). A well-known journalist Shekhar Gupta in **'**CV and stature**'**, commented in 2017, "It was never the quality of the CV that defined an incumbent's performance or legacy. It was that other, unquantifiable quality: Stature. Kalam, Venkataraman, and Narayanan had it. Giri, Ahmed, and Ms. Patil didn't."

From the election of the first President, Dr. Rajendra Prasad, in 1950 to 2022, Presidential elections have been held 16 times. Of these, 15 prominent personalities took the position of the first citizen. Droupadi Murmu is the 15th one.

An Epic Choice

A new chapter was added with the arrival of Presidential candidate Droupadi Murmu in the 2022 elections. Another page of the caste equation had been turned. So far, 6 Brahmins, 3 Muslims, 2 Dalits, and one Sikh, Kayastha and a woman have held the presidency. Respected Droupadi Murmu is the first tribal woman. "Picking up candidates from certain communities and segments of the societies and electing them as the president, is often interpreted as the emancipation and empowerment of that communities and placing them in the larger issue of political mobilisation by the regimes of the day."[1]

Intellectuals and think-tanks find in her an appropriate candidate. They all praise the ruling party and subscribe to the decision. For instance, P R Ramesh wrote, "NDA's decision to elevate Droupadi Murmu as its presidential candidate, against this backdrop, needs to be viewed in the context of the civilisational repair of ancient Hinduism and a new India making a corrective statement that is balanced and inclusive of various communities. It posits a united Bharat, as opposed to one of fragmented identity politics birthed and nurtured for decades after Independence, thus dividing and diminishing the nation. It is a statement whose primary objective is to unite India as a civilisational entity."[2] Professor Makarand R. Paranjape also agreed, "When she travels all over the world as India's Head of State, Murmu will exemplify, contrary to all the negative press, that Narendra Modi, the BJP, and Indian society as a whole, are much more accepting of diversity and much more committed to removing social inequality than many other more so-called advanced nations. That she follows Ram Nath Kovind, a *Dalit* or member of the Scheduled Castes of the Indian Constitution, only strengthens the BJP's social justice credentials. That this government has been bold in breaking with earlier calculations and compulsions is all the more credible."[3]

By nominating Droupadi Murmu, PM Modi has highlighted that the BJP believes in inclusivity and empowering those who have been oppressed for years. BJP's choice of Droupadi Murmu for president is an important signalling for India's historically prideful and underserved tribal communities. PM Modi understands the power of symbolism very well, both in domestic politics and in the country's external projection. Murmu's life trajectory is inspirational and underscores the transformative strength of democracy.[4]

Now we have a tribal community representative leader who happens to be a woman. She is a seasoned politician from Odisha with an extensive background in the field of academics. It is hoped that she will uplift the tribal sections of the country. It is also believed that her arrival will be a plus-point in electoral politics. As Professor Hilal Ahmed of the Centre for the Study of Developing Societies (CSDS), New Delhi has shown in a recent take that "BJP has already emerged as the first choice for Adivasi voters at the national level."

The 64-year-old former school teacher turned politician comes from a nondescript tribal village of Odisha and had a stint as the state governor of Jharkhand. From the PM of the country to the CM of many states, leaders say that she will make 'a great President'. You and I wish her great success!

There was a moment in Droupadi Murmu's life when the Prime Minister expressed the country's trust in her by appointing her as the governor of Jharkhand, a tribal state. Murmu was then asked to visit the villages there. Meet people and listen to their problems. She did the same. Her work as governor was excellent. This was a special reason, due to which she was made the presidential candidate considering her more efficient than other candidates.

When she met the Prime Minister of the country after hearing the news of her nomination for the post of president, she had many questions in her mind. Among them the question she asked first was, "I come from a small village. First I became a teacher and then an MLA and a minister and then a governor, but will such a qualification be enough for the post of the president? Am I eligible for this position?"

The simple reply of the Prime Minister of the country was, "Yes, the country has decided to designate you as her first citizen. The whole country is with you. It is the strength of the people of the country that is with you. And above all, the power given by the Constitution is with you. The Constitution will help and guide you."

Droupadi Murmu accepted this offer to contest elections to make the people of her community and the country proud.

She contemplated, "As the Prime Minister is thinking of bringing Dalits into the mainstream, they should not feel small in life. Those who never got this opportunity after 75 years of independence, who never thought they would reach this stage, are very happy and have lots of expectations. They are very excited. So I said yes to the offer. I have this country, this party and God in my life. So I thought to make the people of the country feel proud. I am dedicating my life to the country. I have accepted the offer not for myself but for the country…" We are also inquisitive and curious to know more about her. Even her name is so unfamiliar to us. She is Droupadi Murmu. Her name is now prefixed *with 'Mahamhim'* and suffixed with *'Mahodaya'*. She will get a few sobriquets in the not-so-distant future. The tribe of her admirers is going to increase at a faster pace than before. Who is she? The other chapters of the book will tell you.

At this stage, it will be worthwhile to know that she faced opposition candidate 'relentless' Yashwant Sinha, a confidante of former PM Vajpayee, in the presidential contest held on July 18. How could an ardent critic of Modi win? It was a losing battle and the opposition was there just trying to seek a political brownie point.

Long Walk to self-actualization

The pages you are going to turn are filled with the story of her long walk to self-actualization. The graceful walk was from Rairangpur in Mayurbhanj District to Raisina Hills in New Delhi. Such a journey takes time, but her voyage took the least. Murmu's journey from being a councillor in a Nagar Panchayat to the President of the Indian Republic was completed in a span of 25 years, from 1997 to 2022. It may amaze you too. Her journey itself speaks volumes about her purposeful life as a polite politician.

She took just 25 years, let me repeat. You may ask, is this because all other presidents were older to her in age? Yes, she is the youngest of them all. All other presidents were born when India was not free. She was born in free India. In short, we can say, she is different. In her difference lies her charm.

There have been so many Madam Prime Ministers and Madam Presidents before too. India made it beginning in 1966. Mrs. Indira Gandhi became Prime Minister of India in 1966. There have been the youngest women heads of state (Finnish Prime Minister Sanna Marin: Finnish Prime Minister in 2019. She is the third woman to lead Finland.) and women heads of government (President Corazon Aquino: the Philippines in 1986). The USA couldn't do so as they faced what a 'pernicious double standard that is aided and abetted by the idea of perfectionism is'. But no other can match Mrs. Droupadi Murmu. She is uniquely placed as she represents what is grand and of an epic proportion in human history. It is a watershed moment in the history of the world. India has taken another step towards becoming a Vishwa Guru. She has already paved the way and created a possibility of future reconciliation and rapprochement for the realization of the dream of New India.

Her Excellency Droupadi Murmu must have realized that she is going to follow in the footsteps of hardworking and disciplined men like Dr. Rajendra Prasad, Dr. Sarvepalli Radhakrishnan, Dr. APJ Abdul Kalam and her predecessor, Shri Ramnath Kovind.

What the then President Shri Ram Nath Kovind had said like a visionary while delivering the speech in the Central Hall of Parliament House on the occasion of taking charge of the office of the President of India on 25th July, 2017 is now on this glorious occasion of Her Excellency Droupadi Murmu taking over worth remembering –

> As a nation, we have achieved a lot, but the effort to do more, try to do better, and try to do faster, should continue. This is also important because in the year 2022, the country is trying to achieve the celebrations 75th year of Independence. We have to keep in mind that with our efforts, the doors of new possibilities and new opportunities open up for that person standing in the last line of the society **and also for that last daughter of the poor family.**[5]

Dreams do come true and predictions too. Droupadi Murmu succeeding outgoing President Ram Nath Kovind will provide two of India's most vulnerable social groups - the Scheduled Castes and the Scheduled Tribes - with an immense emotional satisfaction and an enhanced sense of ownership. How wonderful! A promising daughter of a tribal low-income family is now the President of India!

❐

Chapter Two

From Rairangpur to Raisina Hills

The genesis of a great man depends on the long series of complex influences which has produced the race in which he appears and the social state into which that race has slowly grown...Before he can remake his society, his society must make him.

—Herbert Spencer

JUST DROUPADI

Smt. Droupadi Murmu is the first citizen of India. I am just an ordinary citizen. I write these lines in her honour as I am also amazed like you with the power of Indian democracy. I bow my head in reverence in the memory of those stalwarts who were instrumental in creating a valuable document- The Constitution of India. I tell you the incredible tale of her journey from Rairangpur to Raisina. You and I know what Raisina Hills is but we don't know where this Rairangpur is located. This is the story of a journey which has never been taken before in such a wonderful manner as "The distance travelled by Ms. Murmu, from Rairangpur to the Raisina Hills, is akin to the lonely, tough furrow ploughed by tribal communities in India, who despite being at the forefront of India's struggles against the British colonial rule, had to wait till the Republic's 75th anniversary to get its shot at the top job."[6]

We mortals go on in life without realising what is in store for us. Here is a girl born in a remote tribal village and, by dint of her persistent hard work and dogged pursuit, despite the bouts of bad luck and tragedies, won the most coveted prize. This is the story of a girl singing in school the prayer:

ham honge kamyab ek din
Oh, deep in my heart
I know that I do believe
We shall overcome, someday

Let us know about the present President, the 15th President of India. The life of a person goes on, but there is always a beginning. You too can listen to her spiritual discourses courtesy Youtube and find her narrating her life-struggles in Hindi in a very calm and composed manner. She very often opens up about her life-journey. "I come from the poorest of the poor families and never expected I will take up politics. I had plans to study and get a regular job to support my family financially."[7]

I retell those incidents and I tell them as I got to know, nothing more and nothing less.

Birth and Parentage

Droupadi Murmu was born on 20th June 1958 in Baidaposi village of Odisha in a Santali tribal family. Her father's name was Biranchi Narayan Tudu. Both her father and grandfather were the heads of the village. The Tudu family is called the Sardar family because Droupadi's father, Biranchi Narayan, and grandfather were the heads of the village panchayat. "He gave his daughter a name which was unusual in the tribal community. It was an indicator of the Vaishnavite influence."[8] We all love our names but our names are always 'given'. It is rare that the name is 'taken'. Those who are unfamiliar with her name will not remain unfamiliar. Her name reverberates in all directions now.

In worldly terms, Shri Biranchi Narayan Tudu was just one among the masses. He was a common tribal only. He was neither a freedom fighter nor a rich landlord. He was a plain and simple man, similar to Premchand's rural characters. For him, his entire world was his village and the village was his family. He pursued the supreme value 'The Good' and his daughter inhabited this value from him in abundance.

Uperbeda and Putti of Uperbeda

After a long uneven journey, one can reach Uperbeda, a village with a population of 6623 where Droupadi Murmu spent her childhood. Uperbeda Panchayat has seven revenue villages with a population of 15,000. The population is mostly made up of Adivasi and OBC communities. Uperbeda village has two hamlets- Badasahi and Dungursahi. While Badasahi hamlet is fully electrified, Dungursahi has only 14 households which are yet to get electricity. After the announcements of the presidential candidates, the administration took initiative for electricity connectivity under Saubhagya Yojana. Murmu's nephew Biranchi Narayan Tudu lives at Dungursahi hamlet along with his wife and two children. Her elder brother Bhagat Tudu's son also lives there with his family. Her younger brother Sarani Tudu also lives in the house.

As an MLA and minister, she worked to build 'pucca' roads and a bridge to help people commute with ease. It is very disheartening that there are still 500 villages with no formal roads and 1350 villages with no electricity in Mayurbhanj district. Droupadi was born in this village. She still has her ancestral home here. The old mud house has been painted and looks better than other houses around. The house belonged to Droupadi's father and is now inhabited by her nephew, Dularam Tudu. Dulali Tudu, wife of Dularam Tudu, Murmu's nephew, stays in the village home with their two children.

Uperbeda village is also the birthplace of former MPs Salkhan Murmu, Bhabendra Majhi and former minister Kartik Majhi. Kartik Tudu was also their relative. Once he was a minister who helped Droupadi complete matriculation and study in a college in Bhubaneswar. All this information is widely shared and available on social media from where I collected it. This is to tell you that her blood-relatives and friends are not wealthy landlords. They belong to lower middle class or at the most middle class families. They are hardworking, honest and God-fearing people. They remain satisfied with what they get.

Rairangpur

Rairangpur is a city and a tehsil of Mayurbhanj district of the state of Odisha, India. Rairangpur is 280 km away from Odisha's Bhubaneswar and 267 km away from Kolkata. About 20 kms away from Rairangpur is Droupadi Murmu's native village, Uperbeda. You have to traverse through under-construction roads, uneven hills and dense forest to reach the village. From a nondescript town in one of Odisha's backward regions, Rairangpur will now forever be known as the home of Droupadi Murmu, our 15th president.

Rairangpur can be called a model village or a small town. It is completely digitalized now. At least one person from each home has an account in the bank. It's a development model village for others to follow and the credit of its development goes to the daughter of the village. Now that she is the President of the Indian republic, the entire world will be inquisitive about this remote tribal village. People have also started realising that the daughter of their town has brought them name and fame and now onwards they all will be in the limelight.

(A web-site called 'one India' gives not only her birth place (Baidaposi Village, Mayurbhaj, Odisha) but also her complete address, mobile no. and email. Her Permanent address is- Baidaposi, Ward No-2, P.O. Rairangpur, District- Mayurbhanj pin code-757046. Her contact no is + 9 651 2283469 and email jhrgov@jhr.nic.in I am sure, you will use your discretion and commonsense if you use this information.[9])

According to an India Today report, 'Droupadi Murmu came to Rairangpur in the early 90s after the demise of her elder daughter. Shyam Charan Murmu, her husband, was with Bank of India and the couple shifted together to the house in Rairangpur. Later, she joined a private school for voluntary teaching. She had two more sons, who died at a young age. She has only one daughter, Itishree, who lives with her."[10]

At present, Didi Murmu (She is very fondly addressed by the people close to her as "Didi") lives in Rairangpur's Mahudeeha mohalla. The two-storey modest house has nothing much to show off. The first floor is given to Odisha's Grameen Bank on lease and her younger brother Tarini Tudu and his family live on the ground floor. She also lives there.

You will not miss in Murmu's two-storey house the guest room that is full of framed photographs of her- the ones with the former President, Ram Nath Kovind, and Prime Minister Narendra Modi standing out gracefully.

But when she was born and brought up, the condition of the village was not adequate. It was pitiable. The basic necessities of life were hard to get. People were poor and hand to mouth. Her parents were also not rich enough to provide their children with all the essential comforts of life. But they were all happy and satisfied. They dreamt of happier days and worked hard to come up in life.

In Murmu's early life, the amity and harmony between castes and communities in a tribal setting were exemplary. The village where Droupadi Murmu was born in 1958 is a typical Indian village where people lived together and helped each other to grow along with their national aspirations. The family believed that the key to success lies in being true to oneself.

Tribal lineage

Droupadi's parents belonged to a particular tribe called Santhals. The Santhals are among the major tribes, including the Gond, Munda, Ho, Oraon, Bhil, Mina, Khond, and the Nagas. Santhals, also known as Manjhis, are an ethnic group largely concentrated in the states of Jharkhand, Odisha, Bihar and West Bengal. According to Britannica, there are over 5 million Santhals in India alone. The late Prof. Nihar Ranjan Ray, one of our most distinguished historians, had described the Central Indian Adivasis as "the original autochthonous people of India."

India, despite an 8.6 per cent tribal population, is traditionally known for neglecting this segment. One-third of the world's tribal and indigenous population, that is, over 104 million tribal people live in India. Spread across 705 communities, they represent unique cultural diversity. The tribal population suffers from communicable diseases, non-communicable diseases, malnutrition, mental health, and addictions complicated by poor health. An expert committee on tribal health has given recommendations with the goal to bridge the current gap in the health status of tribal people by the year 2027. Unfortunately, they are not integrated into the national mainstream leading to lower educational levels (41 percent Illiteracy) and economic attainment (41 per cent Below Poverty Line); a life often marred by lack of material circumstances and lack of access to public utilities and services. Their geographically isolated habitats often compound their problems.[11]

Droupadi's family was one among them.

In other words, her family belongs to the Scheduled Tribes. In India, Scheduled Tribes have been identified on five basic criteria: primitive traits, backwardness, geographical isolation, distinctive culture, and shyness of contact with other communities (in 2017, the government deleted the word 'primitive'). It is a category of people who have been subjected to a lot of hardships. Yet, they continue struggling to take their rightful place in Indian society and the political arena. Verrier Elwin, the great anthropologist, said about them, "These are the real Swadeshi products of India, in whose presence all others are foreign. These are ancient people with moral rights and claims thousands of years old. They were here first and should come first in our regard."

All Scheduled Tribes are not adivasis. There are some 573 communities who are recognized by the government as Scheduled Tribes and therefore eligible to receive special benefits. They all compete for reserved seats in legislatures, government jobs, universities and schools. Some get them and some do not. The struggle continues.

It is worthwhile to note that she carries with her a rich culture and an astounding but struggling political legacy. Though the fiery spirit of her people couldn't become a part of our combined lore, there are innumerable tales told by them and those who know them well. It is unfortunate that we have been deprived of that learning. Santhals lost thousands of their kin for the sake of the motherland. They fought with such vigour that British Army officer Major Jervis had to admit, "It was not war; they did not understand yielding. As long as their national drum beat, the whole party would stand, and allow them to be shot down." In England, famous novelist Charles Dickens also discussed the war with Santhals in his weekly magazine 'Household Words'. Praising them for their honourable behaviour during the war, he mentioned, "They are infinitely more respectable than our civilized enemy, the Russians, who would most likely consider such forbearance as foolish, and declare that is not war."

With great valour and civilizational wisdom behind it, Droupadi Murmu was born in Independent India, and in the sixties, she started educating herself as she could. The Constitution of independent India gave her a chance and opportunity to grow. She was born in one of the remotest villages of a less-developed area in a Santhal- tribal family. She became the brightest star of the country, the president of the Indian republic. However, that is the diversion in the story. Let us remain where we were.

Childhood

In an interview with Doordarshan's 'Tejaswani' programme nearly 6 years ago, she hinted about her life-struggles from the very beginning. Anyone can listen to that endearing programme. She very candidly told the interviewer that there used to be small problems to be solved. The family was not so well-to-do that the parents could send their daughter out of the village for further studies beyond school. She wanted to study to stand on her own and it was also in her little smart growing mind to do something for her family too.

I immediately recollected a story by Premchand in which the little boy Hamid was planning to buy a 'chimta' (a pair of tongs) in the village fair for his grandmother. Yes, the story's title is "Idgah" (1933). Grandmothers are really lovely beings in our tiny budding lives. She had a grandmother who knew English too! Her grandmother was educated according to the standards of her days. She was from Chakradharpur. She used to speak Hindi and sometimes a few sentences of English to let her grandsons and granddaughter know that she was not illiterate and knew well the value of education. She used to inspire her granddaughter to learn and study to go forward in life. She was very fond of her little granddaughter as she was named after her. Her grandmother's name was also Droupadi Tudu. But the child Droupadi's nickname is Putti. Children take their elder's words as gospel truth and Droupadi too followed her grandmother's words in letter and spirit. She used to tell her about her progress in class and shared her small dreams too. Grandmother used to tell her stories of velour, uprightness and Dharma.

Primary School in Uperbeda

Child Droupadi studied in the village primary school before moving to Bhubaneswar for her secondary education. Manoranjan Murmu, present principal of the school, says that the school was the only one at her time and was established in 1902, according to school records. The 1971 Census put the literacy rate of the Mayurbhanj district at 12.22%. There were no matriculate (a class 10 qualification) women in Uperbeda, and Droupadi was determined to be among the first.

Midhun M Kuriakose interviewed Vasanth Kumar Giri, a former school teacher at the lower primary school in Uperbeda village. The teacher still remembers the smile on the face of a 4-year-old girl clinging to her father's hand on her first visit to the school.

> Her name was Droupadi Tudu then. She was the eldest of the then village head Narayan Tudu. (She took her husband's surname and became Droupadi Murmu after her marriage to Shyam Charan Murmu, a bank officer.) Narayan left his little girl at school and told me to teach his daughter well. She was smart and came first in all exams. She had the oratory skills of her father. She participated in all the oratorical contests held for students annually and won the first prize without fail. We, teachers, were sure that she would reach great heights and make us proud.[12]

The headmaster of Droupadi's school, referring to the past, said that from 1968 to 1970, he was the head teacher there, when Droupadi was studying in the school. He feels proud to say something about her. The headmaster says that he still remembers well that once students were asked what they wanted to do and become. Many children gave their own answers but Droupadi said that she wanted to serve the people. Droupadi's aunt Saraswati said that Droupadi has proved what women can achieve. She has struggled a lot throughout her life. It is the result of her relentless struggle. She is very humble and grounded in nature. We are always together in happiness and sorrow. In our time, we girls were always told whether we would do it by studying. People used to ask her what she would be able to do. Now she has proved to them what she can do.[13]

(This is the way we weave a story. I have no source to find out the real incident. The happening truth and the story truth are so intermingled that there is no chance to separate one from the other. Let it be.)

She studied from class 1 to 7 in the village school. She was in class seventh then and wanted to study further. But there was no school nearby beyond class seven. She used to discuss this with her parents, who were unable to guide her properly. They themselves were not so much informed about the schools and other facilities outside of the village. They were eager and ready to send her out of the village also if she got admission in the state capital.

A very charming story is told by Journalist and activist Nigamananda Patnaik, who's known her since 1980. She is the only known source of it. Let me give it to you for your amusement, entertainment and learning.

> When she was a child, her father took her to the nearby town of Rairangpur when a minister in the Odisha government, Kartik Majhi, was visiting. Suddenly, she

ran up onto the stage, waving her school certificate, and told the minister that she wanted to study in Bhubaneswar. The minister was so impressed by the little girl's enthusiasm that he ordered his staff to help her get a place in a government school in the state capital.[14]

Another story is told by Rabindra Patnaik, Murmu's family friend of 40 years and a journalist based in Rairangpur, which goes as follows. "In her primary school class, she was the topper in studies and sports. There were 40 boys and 8 girls in her class. As a norm, the topper becomes a monitor, but more than 55 years back, in a patriarchal society, she wasn't allowed to. So she fought hard and became the monitor."[15]

Visit of a VIP

When this kind of daily discussion was going on at home, she came to know about the arrival of some minister in the village. Though the visit of the VIPs was not a rare occasion, she was very happy to know and asked her father to permit her to go there. Her father agreed and told her that she should go herself alone and meet them as he would not be able to talk to them properly. You can understand that the very thought of conversing with government officials sent shivers in tribal- community individuals.

Tribal people fear going to a police station or court. When they see a tribal person at the top post, they have some faith. That was the reason that her father was hesitant to accompany her. He was afraid of those IAS and IPS officers who would be around and dominating. He knew his limitations, but he knew that his daughter would be able to present herself and her problems in the best possible manner. He also wanted to see her go ahead and face the world as it was then.

Her father didn't go along with her. She went alone with her report-card and other important documents and surprised all the officers and the minister with her request and firm determination to get educated. She went into the room and just glanced at all the IAS –IPS officers present. She handed over her certificates to the minister, who promised to extend any help he could and thus, her problem was solved. She was admitted to the school situated in the state capital. The free- hostel facility was another advantage. Thus she studied from high school to her graduation in the city without much bother. She used to get a princely sum of Rupees ten from her father as pocket money. Her brothers, who remained in the village, couldn't go beyond school. Perhaps they were not that much adventurous or they were satisfied with what they got in the village. We don't know.

When there were not even roads to travel and the family was too poor to afford them, she reached Bhubaneswar and studied. She showed the other boys and girls of her area, 'where there is a will, there's a way.' Seeing a girl going to the city and getting an education, some boys also got inspired. After that, so many more students dared to go out of the village and make their way in the competitive world.

In this way, from the very beginning, she made her life an open book to emulate and learn from her example. There are a lot of taboos and social barriers in the Santhal community which prevent young girls and boys from achieving big. There are a lot of stereotypes associated with the tribal and the community needs a lot of outside exposure. Droupadi showed them a way and told them that one of the simplest ways to come up in life goes through the portal of education.

This incident shows that she understood the value of going out and seeing the world outside her village and vicinity. She didn't behave like a well-frog or the proverbial *kupamanduka*. A *kupamanduka* is a frog that lives its whole life within a well, knows nothing else, and is suspicious of everything outside it. It talks to no one and argues with no one on anything. Her world would have been like the world of her brothers had she lived within the confines of her village.

Early Secondary Education

One day in July 1970, Droupadi picked up her bag and joined a girls' high school in the state capital Bhubaneswar, 280 km away. She lived in Kuntala Kumari Sabat Hostel. In the years that followed, she lived in Bhubaneswar, completed her schooling, and studied sociology and political science, joining Rama Devi Women's College in 1974.

Droupadi passed her matriculation from the Unit II Girls' High School in 1974. She studied there for three years (Class 8, 9 & 10). She was quite amiable as a student and had a very good rapport with all the teachers and students.

As a studious girl, Droupadi did not stop after her matriculation examination. She went on and got admission to Ramadevi Women's College in Bhubaneswar, where she completed her IA and BA.

In Murmu's public life, the role of RSS is generally underlined, but they forget that child Droupadi lived and learnt when Congress was everywhere. The governments of the day provided her opportunities to grow. Her formative years witnessed an era in which there was a continuous struggle between "India" and ''Bharat." This is also worth remembering that the Nehru Era, when there was a dream to develop India into an industrialized nation, was different from the Indira regime, in which the leaders were ready to take a broom and sweep her house clean if she asked for it. "India is Indira and Indira is India "kind of slogans became examples of flattery." Droupadi, from her childhood to her youth, lived through it and lived with it. She was born in the Nehru era but lived her entire life beyond it. That is why her admiration for Jawaharlal Nehru, India's first Prime Minister, is well-known. At the start of the first session of the Jharkhand Vidhan Sabha in 2020, she quoted Nehru, "By turning the portraits to the wall, one cannot change the facts of the history."

During her formative year, when after Nehru, his party was taking new strides, the social fabric of her surroundings was also changing. The social workers of different denominations were there to help and inspire the tribal population. Some used to help in return for something. Few ran institutions where charity and good-will were the only motto. The traditions Droupadi saw at home in her village and her surroundings influenced her immensely. She was able to build her character and point of view based on what she went through.

Nelson Mandela's long walk to freedom began from home; Droupadi's long walk to freedom started from the village, which was a part of her home.

Graduation and Marriage

She holds a Bachelor of Arts degree. She graduated in 1979. She studied at Rama Devi Women's College,

Bhubaneswar. The college is a university of repute now. "She was good at studies and would take part in competitions. I remember her playing the lead role in a play," says Santhali litterateur and Padma Shri Damayanti Besra, who was Murmu's junior in college.

Her only goal in life was to study and then get some job so that she could stand on her own feet. She wanted to help her family as they were also not rich enough to get all the comforts of life. There were no great dreams, no profound ambitions, and no hope for some dramatic change in their subdued lives. During her college life also she kept a singular goal of supporting her family. She wanted to support her father financially but couldn't do so as she was married then. In 1979, Murmu got her first job as a junior assistant at the Odisha secretariat. She married on her own will; it was a love marriage. "She married on her own will; it was a love marriage," said Droupadi's brother.

Let me say a few more words about Droupadi's marriage with Shyam. This is a 42 years old love story. She was Droupadi Tudu earlier; Droupadi became Murmu after marrying Shyam. Droupadi was pursuing her graduation from Bhubaneswar. She was good in her studies, otherwise how would she have reached Bhubaneswar after 7th standard. At that time, she was the only girl studying from her village. She studied in a tribal residential school from 1970 to 1973 and then joined Rama Devi Women's College, Bhubaneswar for graduation. During her college days, she met Shyam Charan Murmu, who was also studying in Bhubaneswar. Both fell in love.

After some months, Shyam with his family reached Droupadi's home with a marriage proposal. It happened in 1980. When her father, Biranchi Narayan Tudu, came to know about the whole affair, he got angry with Droupadi. He was not happy with this relationship but Shyam had gone there with a determined mind. He was there with his uncle and two or three other respectable persons from the village. He, along with his relatives, had camped in her village for three-four days.

Droupadi had also made up her mind. It took some time and little persuasion but eventually everyone agreed.

The marriage was confirmed, but the dowry was yet to be fixed. Among the tribals, the people of the boy's side offer dowry. The girl and the boy's family decide how much and what will be the dowry. A cow, a pair of oxen and 16 pairs of clothes were fixed in the dowry and Droupadi's family members happily agreed.

Droupadi Murmu was married in 1980. Everyone knows this, but no one knows the exact date. The house where she came as a bride in Paharpur village is now a residential school. There are about 100-125 houses in this 400-voter village. The people of three tribal communities, Ho, Munda and Santhal live in this village.

Her in-laws were not in favour of her going to work. They wanted her to let the husband and children be looked after and house-hold chores to be done diligently. They indicated if the wife and the husband both go to work; it would not be good for the family and growing children.

Work and Services

After graduation, she joined the Odisha government in a clerical post at the secretariat in Bhubaneswar. She worked there as a Junior Assistant in Irrigation and Power Department from 1979 to 1983. By this time in 1980, she had married Shyam Charan Murmu, who worked at a State Bank of India branch at Rairangpur. Leaving her children behind with her in-laws and husband at Rairangpur, 350 kms away from Bhubaneswar, was not easy. Her in-laws insisted her to leave the job and she had to do so as her children and her husband required her care. She came back and took up a job as a teacher at the Aurobindo Integral School in Rairangpur. She refused a full salary and was content with a paltry sum of money as an honorarium as her idea was to look after and monitor the education of her budding children also. She was the mother-cum-teacher-disciplinarian in the life of her sons and daughter.

Before entering social work and politics, she began her career as a teacher at Sri Aurobindo Integral Education Centre in Rairangpur. The kids were growing up. She had some time to spare. She was looking for work. So she started working as a teacher without pay. Staffer Dilip Kumar Giri who got a chance to work with her, recounts, "I used to look after the management back then. Murmu taught students Hindi, Odiya, Maths and Geography etc., for free. We could see she always wanted to help others. There was so much compassion in her."16 Her daughter Itishree Murmu recalled that her mother was a very hard task-master in the school and was a disciplinarian indeed. "She was my teacher at school as well, so there was added pressure on me. I was her student first and daughter later.

My friends used to be angry on me when my mother used to take these surprise tests."[17]

BJP president J P Nadda compared Murmu with former President Dr Sarvepalli Radhakrishnan. "Like Dr Radhakrishnan, her life also has been closely connected with education. She was a teacher by profession."Sanjay Kumar Mishra from Raipur puts it this way when he says that she not only taught there, but taught herself to be tenacious, all through her life. Despite losing her husband and two sons as a personal tragedy, she persevered to remain cool, in order to look after her daughter Itishree. Beginning her life as an honorary teacher set the ball rolling for her. With humility came wisdom and she crossed many hurdles to climb the ladder of success."[18]

Public Service

She started working with social organizations to uplift villagers hailing from the remotest parts of Odisha. She used to travel far and wide and left no stone unturned in helping them. For her enthusiasm and selfless care of the under-privileged, she had to bear a lot of hardship and comments. It used to be very difficult to serve as a social worker. But she defied odds and cultural stigmas to serve the people. She withstood strongly before cultural and social stereotypes. She was an educated-a graduate from a reputed college and the women around her were illiterate and uneducated. They were fearful of her. So she decided to remain like them. She wore the same type of simple clothes. She spoke the same kind of language. When she entered the political arena and took it as a career in politics, there were certain individuals who found it strange and beyond comprehension. Women were considered ill-equipped to work day and night, travelling far and wide. But she continued serving people unfazed with comments and criticism. Impressed by her work for the socially backward people, there were many philanthropists and intellectually sound persons who felt a spark in her. They persuaded her to take full-time social work which eventually led her to become an MLA and later a minister.

She was always ready to help and guide poor people around her. They were all asking for help in life. They were not even sure if they should not ask for help for personal matters. Her helping nature made others happy and they all praised her. It is said that during those days, a local BJP leader Ravi Mahanta found in her that spark which is the sign of a budding leader. Raj Kishore Das, Biju Janata Dal MLA from Morada constituency in Mayurbhanj district, who was then with the BJP, recounts, "I first spotted Murmu during the early 90s when she taught at the Aurobindo School. I wondered who is this educated, tribal woman is selflessly teaching at a school! I was then the chairperson of the Rairangpur Notified Area Council (declared as a municipality in 2014). In those days, the BJP was trying to get a toehold in Odisha and was looking for dedicated leaders."

There are many helping hands that come forward if the person is willing. Finding her great work in social service and her gaining popularity in the area of her work, the minister who helped her at the initial stage for getting admission persuaded her many times through some lady known to both of them to join politics.

She was a teacher and a social worker. Her reputation as a teacher grew around and her social service was free from any dispute. However, the most important quality was her clean and spotless conduct. She was never part of the ABVP (student organization affiliated to the RSS) during her days in college, but she came close to senior Sangh functionaries after joining the BJP in 1997.

I would say that the most remarkable possession she had at that time was her close bond with the parents of the students she was teaching. They became her messengers and campaigners. Her own modest background helped her in instinctively empathise with the poor. She did not strain herself much to connect with her voters. They were already connected with her. All her students and their parents were big fans of her long before the other voters in the constituency came to know about her humility and humane nature.

She started her political career in 1997. Murmu contested the councillor's election in 1997 and won. She was made in-charge of sanitation work. It was one of the most essential services but highly neglected as many people did not want to take it. But Droupadi accepted it as a challenge. She used to come in her Maruti 800. By parking the car in a distant colony, she would get the cleaning work done under her care. People took notice of her work and appreciated it. It seemed that if she contested the election, she would definitely win.

She was elected Councillor of the district board in Rairangpur in 1997. She has been MLA twice in Odisha and became MLA twice on a BJP ticket from Rairangpur in Mayurbhanj (2000 and 2009). When BJP was losing its sheen with the rise of Naveen Patnaik, she could hold her constituency. She also got a chance to work as a minister in the Naveen Patnaik Government. She held the portfolios of commerce and transport from 2000 to 2002 and fisheries and animal resources development from 2002 to 2004 in Naveen Patnayak's government. She didn't know a bit about the departments and its working but she learnt everything. She was also awarded the Neelkanth Award for a Best legislator by the Odisha Legislative Assembly. Santosh Satpathy, a 1986-batch IAS officer of Jharkhand cadre, who was special secretary to Patnaik in his first term, described Murmu as "extremely dignified with strong values and ethics; she was uncompromising on principles." Satpathy had served as Murmu's principal secretary after she became the governor.

The leadership quality I observed in her way of conducting herself was her ability of taking responsibility and accountability for any work assigned to her. She followed Atal Bihari Vajpayee, who says that man achieves and achieves. The achievement takes him to newer heights but finally to loneliness too. She learnt humility and humbleness from such public figures as Vajpayee ji.

As happens with many busy social workers and leaders, she couldn't give proper personal care to the family and children all the time and became more engaged in social work. Her husband supported her in all her endeavours. She also helped her family in whatever way she could. She helped her mother and brother financially and saw to it that they should live in comfort.

An Anecdote

An example of her simplicity and zeal is exemplified by a BJP worker who met her in 2006 and spent time with her. The story appeared in News18.com on July 05, 2022 by Niloy Bhattacharjee. The name of the BJP worker is Borkotoky. I heard her name first time when I was searching for some inspiring anecdote about Murmu's life. This story is one such in which you will find Droupadi Murmu as an ordinary mortal like you and me. Let me cite the story for you.

> In 2006, Borkotoky, a young grassroots Bharatiya Janata Party (BJP) worker from the tea garden community, had met the then MLA from Odisha Murmu in Bishwanath.
>
> She had come to campaign for Diganta Ghatowar, the BJP candidate. The district BJP office-bearers introduced me to Murmu madam. She was an MLA from Mayurbhanj in the Rairangpur district of Odisha. I stayed with her for seven days. We travelled in the same car with no security.
>
> There was a disturbance in Assam as we moved into the interior of Bishwanath, along the Arunachal border. We stopped by the roadside tea stalls for morning and evening snacks as we went to Majuli and Pratapgarh. She is extremely simple and much organised. We stayed in the same room. She is an early riser. However, she used to wake me up after finishing her morning workout. She was like my elder sister advising me on life and the way of living. I introduced her to Pallab Lochan Das, BJP MP, a young student leader. He invited madam and me for dinner.
>
> Once I took her to a restaurant as she was our guest. She asked me if I wanted to make her ill by feeding her such oily food. After that, we never had food in restaurants.[19]

Political Journey

In a February 2020 interview, she spoke about her political journey: "I started as a teacher without pay and later worked with social organisations to uplift villagers hailing from the remotest parts of Odisha in 1997..."

Droupadi Murmu won her first poll in 1997, becoming a councillor. She was an independent candidate for the Ward No 2 seat in Rairangpur's Notified Area Council, which was a reserved seat for ST women. She later joined the BJP and became Vice Chairman of the council. She was also the vice president of the Scheduled Tribes Morcha of the BJP. Her story is short but not too short to be finished in a sentence or two. She is the 15th President of India. What more one can write or say as if Modi has become the voice of us all. Droupadi Murmu Ji has devoted her life to serving society and empowering the poor, downtrodden as well as marginalised. She has rich administrative experience and had an outstanding gubernatorial tenure, he said. "I am confident she will be a great President of our nation, millions of people, especially those who have experienced poverty and faced hardships, derive great strength from the life of Murmu. Her understanding of policy matters and compassionate nature will greatly benefit our country.

2022: 15th President of the Republic of India

2015-2021 Governor of Jharkhand State

2013: National Executive Member S.T. Morcha, B.J.P. till April, 10th, 2015.

2013: Again Elected as District President, Mayurbhanj (East), B.J.P. till April, 10th 2015.

2010: District President, Mayurbhanj (East), B.J.P.

2007: Awarded as "Nilakantha Award" for The Best MLA of the year 2007 by Legislative Assembly of Odisha.

2006-2009: State President S.T. Morcha, B.J.P.

2004-2009: Member of Legislative Assembly, Rairangpur, Odisha. 2002-2009: National Executive Member S.T. Morcha, B.J.P.

2000-2004: Member of Legislative Assembly, Rairangpur, Odisha and became Minister of State (Independent Charge), Govt. of Odisha, Department of Transport and Commerce.

2002: MLA and Minister, Department of Fisheries and Animal Husbandry 1997: Vice-President State S.T. Morcha, BJP.

1997: Won as Councillor and became Vice-Chairperson Rairangpur

1994-1997 Honorary Asst. Teachers at Sri Aurobindo integral Education Centre, Rairangpur

1979-1983 Served as Jr Asst in irrigation and power Dept. Govt of Odisha

Personal family life: The Tsunami

"It hurts to live after someone has died. It just does. It can hurt to walk down a hallway or open the fridge. It hurts to put on a pair of socks, to brush your teeth. Food tastes like nothing. Colours go flat. Music hurts, and so do memories. You look at something you'd otherwise find beautiful—a purple sky at sunset or a playground full of kids—and it only somehow deepens the loss. Grief is so lonely this way."

— Michelle Obama, Becoming

"2009 mein chunav haar gai bachche shahar mein the main ganv mein rahne lagi... Samaj aap ki wait kar raha hai tapsya karne lagi pravchan dene lagi ganv gavan."

—Droupadi Murmu

In one of the talks on Brahma Kumari's television programme, Murmu herself narrated her life's predicament, "The tsunami came into my life in 2009. It was a huge jolt to me. I couldn't hear anything for a few days. I slipped into depression. *Log kehte the ye to mar jaegi* (People thought she will not survive). But, no, I wanted to live."

Murmu's political career has also not been so easy. After winning two consecutive assembly elections, she lost two consecutive elections in 2009 and 2014. In 2009, she contested the Lok Sabha elections from the Mayurbhanj constituency, but lost due to the breakdown of ties between the BJD and the BJP. The electoral setback was not enough. It was her worst time. As if destiny was angry. There was turmoil in her personal life, everything went like a plunder. Over the next six years, she lost her three closest family members – her eldest son Laxman Murmu in 2009, her younger son Sippan Murmu in 2013 and then her husband Shyam Charan Murmu in 2014. (According to the feature published in Amar Ujala on 19th July 2022, their first daughter passed away in 1984.)

When she lost the election in 2009, she came back to her village and told her sons that she would now stay in the village and take care of the family. Her two sons were studying in the city and she had nothing much as far as financial backing was concerned. She was dependent on her pension. It was a setback that all of a sudden, after defeating in the election, she was on her own in her village. As if that was not enough, her destiny turned from bad to worse.

She lost her eldest son Laxman Murmu. He was only 25. According to a report by Sanam Singh published in 'Jagran', "Draupadi Murmu's life has not been easy; she lost her husband at a young age to the death of two sons. One of her sons Laxman Murmu died in Bhubaneswar on 25th October 2009. He was 25 years old at that time. The night before his death he had gone to have dinner with his friends in a hotel in Bhubaneswar. After returning from there, his health suddenly deteriorated. Then Lakshman in Bhubaneshwar lived with his uncle. He expressed his desire to sleep after returning home. When the door did not open in the morning, the family took him to a private hospital. Where the doctors declared him brought dead.[20]

She lost her second son Sipun in 2013. Sipun was in his twenties. He died in a motorcycle accident. She was completely lost and went into depression. She lost her brother in 2014 and her husband the next year. She joined the Brahma Kumaris Ashram's branch at Rairangpur and started her spiritual journey. Mrs. Murmu continuously missed her two sons and her husband, who passed away and left a vacuum in her personal life. It was a mighty blow. That wasn't easy to fill. According to TOI, "Murmu's life was troubled with multiple personal tragedies. While one of her sons died under mysterious circumstances on 25th October 2009, the other died in a road mishap on 2nd January 2013. Her husband, Shyam Charan Murmu, had died of cardiac arrest. She has a daughter, who is married and settled in Bhubaneswar."[21]

In 2009, when she lost her young son, an engineering graduate, she was crest- fallen and started feeling utter pain and depression. It was such a great blow. Only divine intervention could give her some solace. At this point, she turned to Lord Shiva and turned to spirituality with all her devotion. She had always been a spiritual person and this grave loss made her forget everything and turn to Him. She started recovering and gaining ground somehow.

As if the loss of a son was not the ultimate disaster in her life, the second son also died in 2013. It was a mighty blow indeed. She was at sea. It wasn't easy to survive. She was trying to find some repose in Yoga, meditation and religious discourses. As if God was too cruel to stop, in the same month, she lost her brother and mother too. An ordinary mortal should have fallen flat. She tried to recover. Or God wanted to help her. But the omniscient God had taken away even her husband next year in 2014. Her daughter was the only surviving hope in her otherwise devastated life. She says that her husband was not as strong-willed as she had been; he died as he succumbed to his bouts of depression. In her life, at that time, Happiness was nowhere to be seen. It was darkness everywhere; no light was beaming from anywhere.

Faith was the only thing that she had left with. And she continued. Though she was very upset and distressed and was not able to take party work in right earnest, she was persuaded and convinced by other party workers who knew her well. She was the district party chief and was very popular among party workers and voters. She wanted to leave the party and go to some ashram and take sanyas. It is said that Ram Lal ji, who was then the BJP's organising general secretary, took notice of her plight. Mr Rajkishore Das, her political mentor, adds that the most remarkable part of Ms Murmu's personality "is her equanimity in both happy and sad times and her stoicism in the face of tragedy. The way she gathered herself and continued working for the people even after multiple tragedies in her family speaks volumes about her remarkable strength of character."[22]

Let me add here that Droupadi Murmu shares her lot with Kamala Harris, Vice President of the United States and Joe Biden, the President of the United States, as far as past tragedies are concerned. Kamala lost her mother, Shyamala Gopalan Harris, who died of cancer in 2009 and Joe Biden's son Beau Biden died in 2015 after a brain cancer diagnosis. Human life is so unpredictable indeed!

Murmu has donated her family's land in Pahadpur for public causes. She runs the SLS residential school in memory of her husband and two sons. At the exact location, she has made samadhis in their memory.

Spiritual Solace: Brahma Kumari

Brahma Kumari Ashram gave her a new lease of life. After facing so many tragic incidents that became unbearable and she was in utter pain and dejection, she turned towards *bhakti*. She is a Krishna devotee, Shiv Bhakt and Brahma Kumari disciple. There was a change once she started going to the Brahma Kumaris. She immersed herself in meditation and spirituality at Prajapita Brahmakumari Ishwariya Vishwa Vidyalaya at Rairangpur in the Mayurbhanj district. She has known them since 2002. BK Supriya, the chief in-charge of the ashram, recollects that she was able to come out of her grief and depression through meditation and spiritual healing at the ashram. She is the mother of three (two sons and one daughter) children and the death of two sons made her emotionally exhausted. She was not able to sustain her mental grief. After her first son's death, she didn't talk to anyone or eat properly for six months. She had known the Brahma Kumaris ashram for so many years. She had been a follower and a regular visitor of the Prajapita Brahma Kumari Spiritual University at Mount Abu in Rajasthan. It was natural that she went there and surrendered to the will of God. Murmu's sister-in-law Sukromani Tudu commented, "The sisters at the meditation centre told her that the world was a state and that the souls visited it only for some time."[23]

In 2009, she visited the institute for the first time and learnt Raja Yoga. Since then, she had been in regular touch with it. In fact, she had been part of many programmes of the institute. A long spell of meditation and several sessions of spiritual discourse gave her peace and tranquillity. The meditation technique she learnt from them helped her overcome grave personal tragedies in her life. As a result, her inner self became calm and composed. Her white saree on her nomination day reminds many of her spiritual sides.

She devoted her life to teaching the masses about spirituality. During an event at the Mt Abu centre, Murmu said, "I come here because brothers and sisters are very dear and I take their positivity and vibrations because the atmosphere here is different. When people change by taking advantage of the value-based education of this institution, then India will rise again"[24]

Wasn't it more than a coincidence that Pratibha Patil, who became the first woman President of the country, had also visited the Brahma Kumari Sansthan before becoming the President?

Octavia Paz in his book '*In light of India*' says, "Of course, it is impossible to foresee the future turn of events. In politics and history, perhaps in everything, that unknown powers the ancients called fate is at work." Murmu was devastated in her personal life, but God had something else in store for her. This is Karma.

In the holy book "The Gita", we come across a vivid description of an 'isthit pragya' (stable in the process of maintaining equilibrium), one who keeps a balanced state of mind and loss or gain both does not hurt. She turned herself into an Isthpragya.

Governorship

When the state of Jharkhand was created in 2000 — from the territory that had previously been part of Bihar — Murmu became its first woman Governor (2015-2021). Murmu was sworn in as the Governor of Jharkhand on May 18, 2015. She became the first woman to hold the Governor's office in Jharkhand when she took charge. She was also the first woman leader from Odisha to be appointed Governor of an Indian state.

The BJP faced criticism for choosing a non-tribal as the chief minister of Jharkhand. Her role was to be the chief custodian of the constitution in a state where several pertinent issues concerning development were stuck because of the tribal and non-tribal divide. Her appointment was seen as a balancing act by the federal government led by the Bharatiya Janata Party to appease the state's 8.6 million tribal people. She was also expected to relate and connect better with the locals by opening channels of communication for them with the government. The appointment of a tribal woman as governor in a 5th schedule state was a historic development. Jharkhand State BJP President and MP from Koderma, Ravindra Rai said, the NDA government led by BJP has made a tribal woman leader as governor as part of an effort to give the tribal community of the country their due. This will send a good message not only to the whole country, but also to the world."[25] Governors had been accused of leaning towards the Centre, but Droupadi Murmu was known to be neutral during her tenure. There was an occasion when Murmu, while advising the Raghubar Das government of BJP, returned his bill without any hesitation. November 2016 marked a chaotic period in Jharkhand. The Raghubar Das government of BJP had brought the CNT-SPT Act Amendment Bill. Under this bill, the government wanted to amend the Chotanagpur Tenancy Act (CNT Act) and the Santhal Pargana Tenancy Act (SPT Act) made by the British government to protect the lands of the tribals. The Raghubar government got the bill passed in the House, despite heavy protests and opposition walkouts.

To convert a bill into law, it has to pass through the governor. The bill passed by the government in the House reached the then Governor Droupadi Murmu. Murmu returned the bill to the government without her signature. She questioned the government about the benefit to the tribal community from this bill. The government did not respond and thus the bill could never become a law. The tribal community was very happy with the governor's decision and thanked Murmu. Murmu had said that "around 200 objections were received against the bill, so the question of signing it does not arise." "Mere kalam se koi injustice nahi hoga (I will not let any injustice happen)." The then Chief Minister Raghubar Das had also met Murmu regarding this matter but she did not change her decision. The opposition also praised her for her sensitivity for 'providing a balm to society that was on the boil for a long time.'

She has never been in controversy throughout her tenure. She was always alert on the issues related to tribal affairs, education, law and order, health of Jharkhand. On several occasions, he interfered with the decisions of the State Governments with constitutional dignity and decency. During his tenure as the ex-officio Chancellor of Universities, the vacant posts of Vice-Chancellor and Pro-Vice-Chancellor were appointed in many state universities. Senior Professor at Vinoba Bhave University Prof. Dr Shailesh Chandra Sharma recalls that he himself had organised Lok Adalat on issues related to higher education in the state, in which about five thousand cases of university teachers and employees were settled. In order to centralise the enrollment process in the universities and colleges of the state, he created the chancellor's portal.

"It proves that Murmu can work as per the Constitution withstanding pressure even from the BJP. Generally, women leaders in the BJP get positions and are empowered. So I think Murmu will also get the freedom to work," Smita Nayak, professor of Political Science at Utkal University, told PTI.

She took such bold decisions even during the government of Jharkhand Mukti Morcha. She had managed a good working relationship with Mr Hemant Soren, the CM.

As a governor, she behaved adequately. She presented herself in a dignified manner. She was 'accessible and down to earth' and 'compassionate and balanced.' She used to ask officials to "bring one topic to discuss" with her and "encouraged debate and discussions" on it. "She was fair-minded, soft-spoken and had a good understanding of the administration. She did not interfere in general governance, but when she felt a government did not take the right decision, she would return the bill," says Saryu Rai, who had held several ministerial portfolios in the Das government.

Ratan Tirkey, a former Tribes Advisory Council member, recalls, "While I was the member, the Pathalgadi movement and the attempted tweaking of the tenancy Acts had created distrust among tribal-community. We approached the Governor to hold talks with tribal leaders and take them into confidence for better communication with the government. Sense prevailed and she spoke with the government to do damage control."

Jharkhand's BJP media co-in charge, Ashok Baraik, says: "It was the first time that tribals could easily meet the Governor. She will definitely work to uplift the tribal community in the country." According to BBC Hindi's Ravi Prakash in Ranchi, Jharkhand's capital, Ms Murmu won much appreciation as during her tenure, the governor's office was open to people from all communities and walks of life. An acquaintance from Bhubaneswar remembers her visit when his father passed away. "Droupadi knew my father when she worked as a junior assistant in the irrigation department. She never forgot that he had helped her once."[26]

As the governor of Jharkhand, Droupadi Murmu left an indelible mark and was enormously popular. "She is simple, strong and gentle," is how former Chief

Minister Das describes her. If you call Kalam "People's President', she can be very fondly called a 'people's governor', she was easily approachable. Her five-year term was going to end on May 18, 2020, but was extended. After the completion of her tenure, she left the Jharkhand Raj Bhavan on July 12, 2021, and has been living in Rairangpur since then. Prior to her, no tribal woman had held the position as the governor of Jharkhand. As governor, Murmu received equal respect and camaraderie from both the ruling party and the opposition. This is why Murmu remained in this post until the end of the term. The governor had a tenure of five years but Murmu served for six years, one month and 18 days.

In her long outstanding career, you will find that she neither changed her party nor deviated from the party line. She remained a BJP worker. But once she got the constitutional post of a governor, she declared herself one who was free from party politics. Her life is a lesson to those who are unable to manage successes and failures. She always kept herself calm and composed. She seems to follow the dictum: They also serve who wait and watch.

After her term as governor ended (2021), she returned to her village Uperbeda in the Mayurbhanj district (Odisha) and rejoined her party (BJP) to continue working for the tribal population. She has always been like a guardian to her people. She lives with them as a closed community and they help each other. She has not been attending any political programmes for more than six years after becoming the governor of neighbouring Jharkhand.

One thing that is noteworthy and that should be told is taking a cue from Madhuparana Das' research paper published in 'The Print' on June 23, 2022 that Murmu took BJP head on as Jharkhand governor.

> Murmu's decision to not sign the bill is said to be the reason she was not picked as the NDA's presidential candidate in 2017, when her name was allegedly on the list of probable but (current President) Ram Nath Kovind was finally nominated by the NDA. "Her decision is believed to have cost her the nomination in 2017. In July, just a month after her refusal to give assent to the bills, NDA announced the name of the presidential candidate. But she was not overly ambitious. These are the qualities that made the Sangh believe that her name should be pushed as a nominee this year.[27]

CHARACTER AND CHARACTERISTICS

A follower of Mahatma's footprints

On several occasions, she underlined the contributions of Mahatma Gandhi, Pt. Nehru and Ambedkar. For instance, at the convocation ceremony of the National University of Study and Research in Law, Ranchi, she mentioned each of them and their contribution in the making of the Constitution. They have been her role-models. Among them, Gandhi has been her favourite. Being a Brahma Kumari (a member of the spiritual order of Om Mandali) herself, she spreads a message of non-violence while working to educate tribals and make them self-reliant. Other than this, she, as a woman and as a tribal woman, knows the value of working for growth and empowerment. Handicraft is the way of life for tribal people. They devote their free time and extra energy in spinning and weaving cloth with amazing patterns and designs. As a Governor of a tribal state from a nearby tribal state, Murmu did her bit to inspire people of all strata of life in the arts and crafts. For this, she took the idea from Mahatma Gandhi's way of leading a life amidst nature and her bountiful gifts.

Mahatma Gandhi once said, "For me, nothing in the political world is more important than the spinning wheel". In 1946, Bourke White met Gandhi to film his activities for 'Life' magazine and wrote, "Spinning is raised to the heights almost of a religion with Gandhi and his followers. The spinning wheel is sort of an Icon to them. Spinning is a cure all and is spoken of in terms of the highest poetry.

During her tenure as the Governor of Jharkhand, she got the state's largest spinning wheel weighing 400 kg, built and installed on the Raj Bhawan premises. She is a strong advocate of economic freedom and non-violence, especially for women. Her thing behind the construction of the spinning wheel was that people visiting the Raj Bhawan could learn the value of self-reliance by taking inspiration from the biggest symbol of economic self-reliance. It was inaugurated on August 3, 2020, during Corona time and it is being appreciated as it is one of the five large-sized spinning wheels in India.

She took extra interest and initiative in getting the statues of brave martyrs who laid their lives at the altar of the motherland installed. The statues of Tilka Manjhi, neelamber-pitambar, Telanga-Khadiay, Gaya Munda, Veer Budhu Bhagat, Sido Kanhu, Tana Jatra Bhagat, Albart Akka and others were installed. The Yogmudra Statue of Swami Vivekanand also attracts visitors and the credit for these initiatives goes to her.

A Quiet Conscientious Worker

Those who come in contact with her in different capacities have one thing in common to say about her. She is a quiet worker who never shows off her achievements. She is a great learner and learning by doing is her mantra. When she became a minister of state (independent charge) in the departments of Transport and Commerce, Animal Husbandry and the Department of Fisheries, she hardly knew about the working of the ministry. She was at sea. But she saw to it that her use of good faith and genteel behaviour doesn't send the wrong signal. She was "known to keep her head down and did not get involved in partisanship or fissures between the old and the new guard within the dominant BJD and quietly did her work."[28]

Simplicity and Humility

I don't shout or jump about

Or have to talk real loud.

When you see me passing,

It ought to make you proud.

Does one get her manners and antiquate from her clan? Mrs Murmu is a santhal. It literally means a calm, peaceful person. Santha means calm, and ala means a person in the Santhali (santhal – santal/ santhali-santali are different spellings of the same word). By nature, Santhals are calm and peace-loving people. She has also got her simplicity, calmness and poise from her culture and upbringing.

Her simplicity is not only in her rural looks and effortless attire; it is a mark of her lifestyle. This simplicity can be felt in her living and conducting both in her conduct of personal routine and government business. Droupadi Murmu's brother, Taranisen Tudu, said in an interview, "She is very simple. Her simplicity defines her. She gets up early, meditates, goes for her morning walk, and does Yoga. Even during her time as a governor; she only ever used a car that her daughter gifted her, indicating her personality."[29]

Her simplicity and humility were felt by all when we saw her sweeping the premises of Lord Shiva's temple to offer her thanks to the Lord for her nomination for the Presidential Election.

Kabi Vishnu Satpathy, who has known her since the 1980s, describes her as a "straightforward and simple" person."A compassionate woman, she's good at heart, with no arrogance, no airs. She doesn't show off, mixes freely with people and is humble and down-to-earth. As a politician, she knew how to take people along."30 When she was Governor, she did not get herself trapped in the paraphernalia of governorship. She led a simple life devoid of an army of personal servants and helpers. She has never been in favour of personal security guards. Nitin Madan Kulkarni, Principal Secretary (PS) in the Jharkhand government who was earlier PS to the Governor, said, "She is very humble. Once the aide-de-camp accompanied her to her house in Rairangpur, but there was not enough space for the officer, so the Odisha government had to make arrangements for his stay while Droupadi ji stayed in her house. Such was her simplicity."[31]

"When she was an MLA, she used to travel in night buses from Bhubaneswar to Rairangpur so that she could stay close to the people of her constituency and also attend assembly on time. In her food, clothes, and everything, you will only find simplicity. After she retired as governor of Jharkhand in 2001, she loved spending time with her grandchildren."[32] This is the way her daughter puts it about her simplicity.

Vegetarian and Satvik

Droupadi Murmu is not only vegetarian but also restricted to satvik food. She does not even eat onions and garlic. When a guest comes to her house, the same food is served to him. Her favourite food is Pakhala, a local watery dish made of rice and curd. House Controller S S Parihar, who is in charge of running the Raj Bhavan operations, recounts that when Murmu first came as Governor, she directed that only vegetarian food would be cooked in the kitchen but made exceptions for the guests and her staff. Recalling an instance, Parihar says: "Then Home Minister Rajnath Singh had visited Raj Bhavan once and ma'am got to know that he ate fish. So the food was prepared in a separate place. But when Rajnath ji got to know that ma'am ate only vegetarian food, he insisted that he too would eat the same."[33]

Strong will-power and determination

Jab saare darwaze band ho jate hain, tab bhi wo patience nahin chodti.

(She remains patient even though there is chaos all around).

Ms. Murmu belongs to a member of the Adivasi community of Odisha, a particularly marginalised group in India. "She has shown tremendous willpower and self-determination. She has immense patience. She never gets restless and annoyed. Even at the time of great personal loss, when any other person would have been shattered, she showed exemplary composure. She doesn't panic easily and always believes that this too shall pass. With her strong willpower and determination, she has overcome many challenges, both personal and professional."[34] This is how her 35 years old daughter Itishree describes her mother's salutary qualities.

Similarly Droupadi Murmu's uncle who was a manager in a bank says, "She is an emotional person but a firm woman. She is a *jiddi* (stubborn) woman. Her determination is strong. Don't underestimate her capacity. She is well-read, can give speeches and understands what's good for the tribal community. She has a strong sense of self-pride. Don't call her a 'rubber-stamp'."[35]

Not active on Social Media

Murmu's personal assistant Suraj Kumar Mahato said that she does not have any Twitter account. All the accounts being circulated in cyberspace in her name are found to be fake. As of now she is not present on any social media platform. When Prime Minister Narendra Modi tweeted her congratulated message, he did not did not tag any Twitter account in his tweet.[36]

Plain and Simple

She is not a very articulate person. She speaks as if she is in conversation with the others. She does not evoke bhakti or devotion towards her. No one can claim that she has a charismatic personality. She does not fit well in the definition of an overpowering and mesmerising leader. She is not like Birsa Munda, who inspired generations. Her social work stint is also limited and her political leaning is without any aggression. Yet, she has her own charm. Her work and deeds should be viewed with reference to the social sphere she lives and lived. Lastly, now that she is the President of the Indian Republic, her contribution will be assessed and examined by historians and intellectuals accordingly.

It did not lower her determination to continue to live for the poor people around her. She had her unspent pension with which she was determined to use for the public. She used whatever money she had to build a school. This is also an example of her simplicity and commitment towards development and education. She was not even aware that her name was going to be considered and announced. She heard the news through a TV announcement. "We had met her on the night of the announcement. She told us, 'Aap logon ki kripa se (It's with your blessings)'. Didi was one of us all these years, through her rise in politics, becoming a minister and then governor. But now there will be protocols once she is in Rashtrapati Bhavan," says Kuanar Giri, a neighbour from Rairangpur.

Deeply spiritual, highly religious

Her day starts with prayer and her daily activities come to a close with a prayer on her lips. She is a deeply religious lady.

After receiving the good news along with friends and some family members, she visited the temples of Lord Jagannath, Hanuman and Shiva in Rairangpur, the place from where she was first elected as an MLA in 2000. She also visited Prajapita Brahma Kumari Ishwariya

Vishwavidyalaya in Rairangpur. She swept the premises of the Purandeswari Shiva temple before offering prayers.

Before all this commotion and activities, at the early hours of the day, she reached the Shiva temple in her locality in this nondescript tribal-dominated town called Rairangpur, situated in the Mayurbhanj district. She offered her prayers at the temple. Before the puja, she took a broom in her hand and swept the temple floor clean. When it was certain that he would become India's first citizen, Giani Zail Singh said with glee and gratitude that he would gladly sweep the land on which Indira Gandhi had stepped. It's a difference. Now, after getting the news of becoming the candidate for the first citizen of India, she sweeps the broom inside the temple of God.

It was 3-4 am, then. Nothing unusual. It was also not unusual when she whispered into the ears of Nandi, the Bull 'vahana' of Lord Shiva. I can very well imagine that she must have profusely thanked God and asked Nandi to convey her heartfelt thanks to his master.

After two other temple hops, she visited a tribal worship place called 'Jahira'. Santhals worship their favorite Shalagram. Sal trees are called shalgrams. People of Santhal community worship this tree. Along with the shal, there is an area of about one acre filled with some other trees, it is called Jahira, i.e. place of worship. Speaking to the media, a soft-spoken Murmu thanked them for coming but politely refused to comment; stating that she herself received the news from the television like everyone else. The entire country was so impressed with her devotion that one of her fans from Tamilnadu wrote in "The Hindu", "I am reminded of our Tamil Nayanamars as narrated in Peria puranam. We are sure after settling down, she would visit temples in the South, especially TN being revamped by our CM. She may even write padalgals on Thillai Nataraja in her own mother tongue." The other one went a step further and called a spade a spade, "It is good to see that time has changed and leaders are not scared to practise their Dharma and wear it on their sleeves. Her prayers to Lord Shiva and Nandi ji will act as a death nail against the conversion rackets luring tribals into their folds, brainwashing them as non-Hindus and indiscriminate identity."[37]

Down to earth

She is down to earth. When we say this, you may not understand it well unless some example is given. Let me make my point clear. She doesn't have airs about herself. No arrogance, no haughty behaviour, no tantrum and no complaints whatsoever. She remains on this earth. When the media flashed the news of her nomination and she also came to know about it, she was also amazed like others. Let me dramatise it a little bit to add some entertainment and excitement if I can.

It was the next morning. How fast time flies. She was born on 20th June. The news of her nomination was the perfect birth-day gift for her from the grateful people of India.

Her personal life has not been a bed of roses. That is why when she got the news of her nomination, her happiness knew no bounds. She too got to know about her candidature from television news. She was not expecting this. As she was not in the thick of active political life after becoming the governor of the neighbouring Jharkhand, she was not keeping a tab on the happenings in Delhi regarding the presidential nomination. The reporters who thronged around her could see the joy on her face. She said she was both delighted and surprised by the announcement. She said politely, "I am surprised as well as delighted. As a tribal woman from remote Mayurbhanj district, I had not thought of becoming the candidate for the top post."

This is a scenic representation. Now the solid facts and reliable comments put forward by those who write and get published. Calling Murmu as "an able, empathetic, down-to-earth person", Romita Dutta (June 24, 2022) has very poetically depicted her –village surroundings as follows.

> Chances are you would find Murmu engaged in household chores, quite possibly brooming away fallen leaves from the concrete path leading to the main gate of the house. Once inside, Murmu would make you comfortable, wiping her turmeric-stained hands on a piece of cloth she carries like an apron, and ask you if you preferred normal tea over black. Even after retiring as the governor of Jharkhand in 2021, the affable, ever-smiling Murmu does much of the household work herself. Often, she herself makes the tea served to guests.[38]

Love for learning

She gives a lot of importance to education and learning. The key to success in life is knowledge and so she teaches everyone the power of knowledge. As a school teacher, she learnt and taught the new generation of the tribal population that their all-round development will be ensured through education. So she makes her life an example for others. Her life's mission is education for growth. Her daughter says that her mother used to be very strict as a teacher and never allowed even her daughter to procrastinate. In her speeches too, we find that she wants every child- preferably every girl-child to get an opportunity to study. She is of the view that each citizen of India is a nation builder and each one of us is a custodian of India's well-being and of the legacy that we will pass on to coming generations. That is why a digitally literate, industrialised India is her vision for the future. Educating every girl-child is not only her dream but also her mission and she has been diligently pursuing it. The establishment of a girl's educational institution is an indication that it is her firm commitment. When she met the PM once, she requested him to help her build an educational institution with the pension money she was left with. She is said to have converted her residence in Pahadpur, a village in Mayurbhanj's Kusumi block, into an ashram, where poor kids are imparted English-medium education. Here is an extract from the speech delivered by her as the governor on July 5, 2015. The translation is mine.

> Education is very important in the life of every human being. It is important in personal and social development. Education is a powerful medium in the establishment of a developed society. One should never run away from hard work and hard work to get an education. Education develops the personality and character of a person. It is only through this that serious attention can be paid towards the development of capabilities, possibilities, etc. It is a powerful medium in the direction of inculcating a sense of responsibility in human beings. Education gives a sense of right and wrong. Through this, we can

earn successes in the direction of eradicating poverty and ignorance.[39]

As a governor, she focused a lot on education, particularly for tribals, and ensured the setting up of the Jan jaati bhasha (tribal languages) department at Ranchi University.

Her views on different subjects align with the BJP philosophy and thinking. She is a votary of her language but also favours Hindi. In a video conference held on October 15, 2020, she said, "Ek Hindustani ko kam se kam apni bhasha, yani hindi to aani hee chahiye saath mein hamein hindi ka samman karna seekhna hoga." (Every Indian should not only learn Hindi but also learn to respect the language.")

Her love for learning is not restricted to mere lip-service. During her governorship, she visited all the Kasturba Vidyalayas (Centre-run residential schools for girls from weaker sections). She was always eager to communicate with the girls so that they too get inspired.

She has also opened a residential school in Paharpur village of Odisha for children from economically weaker sections. She is a frequent visitor to this girls' school, run by the family-run SLS Trust (based on the initials of sons Sippan and Laxman and husband, Shyam Murmu). While talking to the Prime Minister once, she had taken the advice to spend her savings in this school. Union Home Minister Amit Shah has very succinctly underlined her love for learning and education when he says that Droupadi Murmu ji has made a special identity in public life by spreading awareness about education in the tribal society and serving the public for a long time as a public representative.

Self-respecting person

In most of her speeches before tribal audiences, Murmu says, "Remember we are equals. Apne ko chota nahin samajhna (Don't consider yourself inferior)."

Her only desire and wish is to work with the best of her knowledge and ability wherever she works and whatever she does. "*aatm-samman*' or '*self-respect*' is her only goal. She is very careful in discharging her duties so that her conduct remains free from any complaint. When she lost the election in 2009, she didn't panic or worry. She took it in her stride. She reached home and started doing social work. It was an example of 'work is worship'. She didn't wander around the corridors of power to get some favours for her and her family. She lived a dignified and settled life.

Tribal people are very honest. Droupadi Murmu narrates an incident as a proof of this. While being an MLA, she once went on a tour of a village in Odisha. There the tribals made them aware of their problems. Some applications were also given. But when she reached there again a few days later, she was stunned to see that many of the same issues remained unsolved. When asked why they had not told earlier, they all remained silent. Murmu knows that tribals are very honest. She opines and her opinion reflects her own personality too, "They will not stand in front of you, again and again, to ask for anything. Of course, their faces are not as beautiful as they look, but they are very clean, honest and innocent of hearts. Pradeep Shukla has brought many such stories and memoirs for 'Jagran'.

Inspired and Inspiring person

Mrs Murmu inspires. Her life is a lesson. She was stuck in the sea and tumult of her personal life. It was such a tragedy that Thomas Hardy could write a Booker-winning novel. In her personal life, happiness has been but an occasional episode, yet she could overcome it with her own inner strength. Her husband failed to withstand the great pain of losing their sons and left this *bhav-sagar*. She stood amidst the tempest, wavering little and withstanding tempests. Ultimately the cruel destiny was defeated and the Gods were pleased again. They were so pleased that they gave her the fittest boon without her asking and desiring it. She has this to say that there must be a fire inside us to win. Everyone has something good and great and we should never think about ourselves as inferior to anyone. She believes in God and her belief gives her the strength to sustain and continue growing and going ahead. Her life-lesson is worth following. It should be part of a moral science curriculum.

Junun hona chahiye. Sab ke andar koi n koi visheshata hai kabhi bhi apne aap ko infiiyar nahin samjhna chahiye. Ichchca shakiti ko thoda majbut karna chahiye, koshish karte rahen ki jeevan mein aage badhe hain

Second Kalam in the Making

Her nature and personality largely resemble that of former President Dr. APJ Abdul Kalam. Becoming 'Kalam' is not easy, yet her life has been somewhat like that of Dr. APJ. It has not been so easy for a woman to reach here after coming out of a remote tribal society. First, you will find just as Kalam loved children and used to motivate the students to move forward; similarly, Droupadi Murmu is also fond of children. She often used to visit schools and colleges while being governor. It was her dogged pursuit that is why the condition of Kasturba Schools in her area improved substantially. She also understands the importance of education, like Abdul Kalam. In 2016 she got Lok Adalats for universities functioning and started the chancellor portal. Only after this other processes, including enrollment in universities, could start online. She had been constantly in touch with the Vice Chancellors through video conferencing. The recruitment of teachers of tribal and regional languages of Jharkhand, which was closed for a long time, was restarted because of her persistent efforts. Last but not the least, she began her career as a teacher and Dr APJ ended his life as a teacher.

Secondly, Just as Dr. APJ Abdul Kalam faced poverty, in the same way, Droupadi Murmu also faced financial and social difficulties. Thirdly, both vouched for simplicity. Droupadi Murmu keeps her life simple and unadorned. He had never been greedy for comfort and luxury. She is always seen in simple attire as if a Mother Teresa of a Brahma Kumari is walking gently. Both disliked paraphernalia. When Droupadi Murmu became M L A for the second time in 2009, she did not have any vehicle and her total deposited capital was only 9 lakh rupees. She also had a liability of four lakh rupees then.[40]

Dr. Kalam had no house, no money, no car and nothing. Even after becoming the President, that simplicity was visible in his walk and talk. He had brought two suitcases to Rashtrapati Bhavan and took only two suitcases when he left the office. Draupadi Murmu also probably follows

Dr. Kalam. She could have lived in any metropolitan city if she wanted, but she has been living in the village of her home state for many years after her governorship. She dislikes pride and pelf. Even after becoming a governor, she neither changed her nature nor dress.

Itishree: All praise for her mother

Let me tell you something about her 35 years old daughter at the end of this chapter. I placed her in the end as etymologically her name means 'the end'. The chapter is being closed and as the famous English poet T S Eliot said- What we call the beginning is often the end. And to make an end is to make a beginning. The end is where we start from." This is the end of the chapter, but the new chapter will begin now.

Let me come to the point. Itishree is the name of our President's daughter. Itishree is Mrs Murmu's daughter, the apple of her eyes. She is with her. She is around her. She speaks for her.

Itishree Murmu is the only daughter of Droupadi Murmu. The proud daughter once had two brothers. But both passed away tragically, leaving her to be the only child in her family. Her father is also no more.

She is married to Ganesh Hembram and settled in Jharkhand. She works in UCO bank. Her husband is a rugby player. She is blessed with two daughters. The elder one is named Adyashri. She was born in 2021. She is now about 18 months old. The second daughter is three months old. Iti's mother is quite attached to her elder granddaughter. Itishree often posts pictures of her mother, daughters, and friends. Her life on Instagram is lively and lovely. Likewise, she is sparsely available on Twitter also.

Itishree Murmu was attending to her three-month-old daughter when she received congratulatory calls from well-wishers and relatives confirming the news she had been longing to hear. She says that her mother broke down when she was informed of her candidature. "She has come a long way in making her way till here, on her own, breaking all social stigmas. When she had gone to study in Bhubaneswar before the nineties, there were no roads, no Google Maps to help people. She figured everything out on her own... She wants to give back to the people of India and to the tribal community."[41]

In an elaborate interview with Subhashish Mohanty, Itishree expressed her joy and elation as it marked the culmination of her mother's career that saw her rise from a ward councillor to the governor to the highest office. On her own plans and whether she would quit the job, the daughter in her said:

> My mother, who is my teacher, would not prefer that I should quit my job; instead, I will apply for a transfer to Delhi... I will watch my mother closely at Raisina Hill and try to emulate her. My mother, who remains calm, always will remain an inspiration not only for me but for crores of tribals in particular. Her struggle to cope up with life will remain an example for generations to come.[42]
>
> My mother has always strived to serve the public, irrespective of the role assigned to her. She created her own ladder of success and kept climbing through hard work. She had never thought of becoming President but kept working diligently. She has a lot of patience. Jab saare darwaze band ho jate hain, tab bhi

wo patience nahin chodti. (She remains patient even though there is chaos all around). Patience and staying down to earth are some of the qualities I have learnt from her. There are a lot of taboos and social barriers in the Santhal community which prevent young girls from achieving big. There are a lot of stereotypes associated with the tribal and the community needs a lot of exposure. Hopefully, my mother's story will serve as an inspiration to the Santhals and also help in our upliftment.[43]

Droupadi 'Didi'

These sentiments of delightfulness, pride, and trust echo across the streets and villages of Rairangpur municipality in Odisha's Mayurbhanj district. She is very fondly called 'Didi' by her supporters and local people. The women of Uperbeda village praise and appreciate Droupadi Murmu and her constant social service for the betterment of the village. A Villager says, 'Hey Droupadi toh humko kaki maa hai." Another says, "I am called by her Aunty." An elderly lady says, "Murmu is the daughter of every family. Whenever she comes, she does not leave without meeting people. She also eats food while sitting at our home. Droupadi has a very humble nature."

A photograph can be seen in which Droupadi Murmu is tying a Rakhi to Odisha CM Naveen Patnaik back in the year 2000 when she was the MLA from the BJP and both Biju Janata Dal and BJP were alliance partners. "He is Jagannath and I am his Subhadra. My brother had given me the gift of support even before I sought it. He also spoke to me over the telephone while he was abroad. I am a village girl and I was a minister. I have done a lot of work."

Let me add that for Patnaik, Droupadi Murmu's election as the 15th President of India is really "a proud moment" for his state. A tribal woman president fits well with his ideal of women's empowerment. In the last General Election, he had sent a self-help group worker, Pramila Bisoyi, to Lok Sabha from his old seat of Aska.

Even the Chief Minister of Jharkhand Hemant Soren addresses her as "Didi'. When Draupadi Murmu was the governor of Jharkhand, she had a very close and family relationship with the Hemant Soren family. Many such occasions came when Chief Minister Hemant Soren, along with his wife Kalpana Soren went to Raj Bhavan and honoured Draupadi Murmu by going beyond the protocol. Former Jharkhand Mukti Morcha (JMM) MLA Prahlad Purty said that he had a cordial relation with 'Didi' Droupadi Murmu. "I have had very cordial relations with Didi (Murmu). Even with her being a Minister and I from the Opposition, she was always very approachable. She has worked for the betterment of the 'Adivasi' community at large. We have been associated with the Jharkhand movement and hence, irrespective of party lines, we are unified when the time has come for the betterment of our people."[44]

On her Name and Surname

Name: Droupadi

Readers! I beg your pardon, if you find this unnecessary and tiresome. I am known for my loquaciousness. My attempt is just to understand and make you understand that there is a meaning in everything including her name.

If I cite Jacques Derrida's views on the name, my book will become an exercise in philosophical musings. If I mention filmmaker Ram Gopal Verma and his tweet, it will be an exercise in futility. But I find it attractive to discuss her name. In French, we say- Sur le nom. It is not out of place. It has cultural significance too. It will be an exercise with epic-proportions. Her father, Biranchi Narayan Tudu, was a farmer. He gave his daughter a name which is unusual in the tribal community. It was an indicator of the Vaishnavite influence. In our scriptures, a lot of importance is given to name and namkaran sanskar. It is said that a contradiction will result with regard to 'Word', we say that it is not so because the origination of everything is from perception and inference (Brahma Sutra, 1.3.28).

Can we start with her name- her first name? Droupadi or Draupadi (both the spellings are being used by the print media). The name of the president reminds me of a Sanskrit sloka my dear departed father used to very religiously recite every morning.

ahalyā draupadī sītā tārā mandodarī tathā |
pañcakanyāḥ smarennityaṃ mahāpātakanāśinīḥ ||

Ahalya, Draupadi, Sita, Tara and Mandodari

One should forever remember the panchakanya

Those are the destroyers of great sins.

Practising Hindus, especially Hindu wives, remember the *Panchakanya* in this daily Morning Prayer. Their names are extolled and the prayer is prescribed to be recited in the early hours of the morning. The *panchakanya* are regarded by one view as ideal women. George M. Williams remarks, "They are not perfect but they fulfil their dharma (duty) as mothers, sisters, wives and occasionally leaders in their own right."

The first name of our respectable President is included and has been taken from in *Panchkanyas*. I needn't remind my able readers that the name and her deeds are part of Indian folklore and she is one of the prominent characters in the classical epic 'The Mahabharata.' The name of the 15th President is so pure and pious that those who utter it will be free from sins. This may look strange to so many and the Indian belief systems are open for discussion, debate and decide kind of platforms. If you feel that this is just out of focus. Never mind, let us discuss, think and move ahead.

Our parents give us our names. Hindus have *naamkaran sanskaar*. Her name is not her choice. It is given. She also got her name from her parents. To put it differently, we can say that she is her father's daughter, as the legendary Droupadi was of her father Drupad.

Surname: Murmu?

This is the last name attached with her first name-Droupadi. This has significance. Let us explore and find out. Her father's surname is "Yudu'; it seems this name (Murmu) is not her maiden name. It is her husband's surname she got. Anyways, let us find out. As the 'surname' as 'nickname' can supplement a given name to the point of replacing it, and in some cases, the surname or nickname seems to have altogether supplanted the given first name, it will be appropriate that we cast at least a cursory glance on her sur-name forgetting what the "Bard of Avon' said, "What's in a name?"

When you look at Wikipedia, they tell you that Murmu is an Indian surname indicating a particular clan of the Santhals. A long list of those great persons who excelled in society is also given. For instance, Girish Chandra Murmu (1959-) is the 14th Comptroller and Auditor General of India. Sidhu Murmu and Kanu Murmu were great freedom fighters. In 1855, the Murmu Brothers led a movement of liberation, which turned into a full-fledged war between the Santhals and East India Company's army. Their memories were honoured by the Vajpayee Government. Did we know?

The fact of the matter is that her family's association with three major tribal communities- Murmu, Tudu and Hembram- made her even more familiar with tribal issues. She has worked really hard for their well-being and to protect their culture and language.

Droupadi Murmu's Kundali

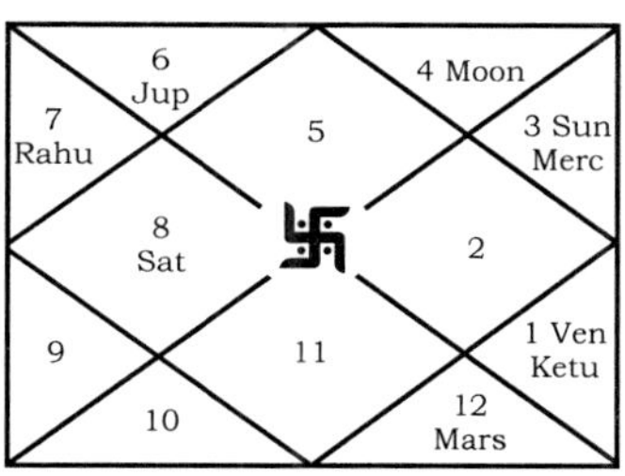

Chirag Bejan Daruwalla says there are some Raja Yogas in the kundali (horoscope) of Droupadi Murmu which can make her successful in her life. In her birth chart, the main zodiac is Pisces and its lord is Jupiter, which is the house of the Guru. Jupiter is in the seventh house in her birth chart and the Lagna Yoga formed by it further forms Samsaptak Raj Yoga. This will bring happiness in her political life. Chirag Daruwala says that the planet Mercury, which is situated in its own house, i.e. in her fourth house, establishes Bhadra Raj Yoga which comes in the category of five great men and strengthens her personality. Because of this, she will be a famous and strong ruling personality. Children will give tremendous motivation to Droupadi Murmu to set goals and achieve them. Droupadi Murmu is a sensitive and emotional person. The harsh realities of this world have a greater effect on her than others, and as a result, she loses some of the joy of life. Draupadi Murmu's nature is calm and this quality gives the impression of being strong and determined in the eyes of others. She does not say as much as she thinks and keeps weighing the pros and cons of the situation.[45]

❐

Chapter Three

The significance of being Droupadi Murmu

Smt. Droupadi Murmu ji has devoted her life to serving society and empowering the poor, downtrodden as well as the marginalised. She has rich administrative experience and had an outstanding gubernatorial tenure. I am confident she will be a great President of our nation.[46]

—Narendra Modi

What they couldn't he did

This is the beginning of the story of our fifteenth President's nomination and subsequent victory. It started and gained immediate public attention when none other than the Prime Minister of India used his official Twitter account and sent a congratulatory message. The proposal of her name for the ultimate position brought tears of joy in the eyes of those who read the message. It was the victory of our democracy and also a message to all of us that India belongs to each and every citizen irrespective of caste, creed, religion and faith. This is a story worth telling and worth reading. Everyone should read it. This story is for We, the People of India.

Even Mahatma Gandhi couldn't imagine then that one day when the people of India would be celebrating their seventy-fifth year of Independence, such an announcement would be made by the then Prime Minister of India. Mrs Murmu's journey to Raisina Hill from Rairangpur can also be seen as an allegory and is symbolic of the struggle of the tribal people to find a place in the mainstream of the nation.

Swapan Das Gupta thought that Modi is attempting to add 'by the poor' leadership to 'for the poor' programmes. But Prime Minister Narendra Modi did what no one thought. He saw to it that a sister of a tribal society sits in the highest office of the country, becomes the President and becomes the head of the three armies was unthinkable. The PM has changed the thought-process of the elite-class. A miracle has happened. Earlier it used to be that a person born in a big family, highly sophisticated, educated abroad, and a well-to-do person of eminence adorned the seat of the President. Today an ordinary woman born into a poor family becomes the President. Did somebody ask for Tilka Majhi earlier? Did anyone know Biju Shyam before? The tribal art and artists, their literature and litterateurs, dance forms and dancers used to be a matter of curiosity and wonder. The talent in them lived untapped and dormant. These are the forgotten people of our tribal society, whom our Prime Minister Narendra Modi is selectively honouring and giving them a share in the administration, government and everywhere. They amply deserve it. Needless to say, her Presidential nomination was appreciated by all sections of society. The tribal society also felt very proud of her candidature.

I have already indicated the nomination. Now let me tell you what Gandhi wanted us to do as soon as India became free. This is very important to know. At a time when the political parties are breaking their heads and trying to choose the most suitable nominee for the Presidential pools, let me tell you what Mahatma wanted us to do as soon as we found ourselves ready to choose our first president in independent India.

Gandhi said this on 2nd June 1947 at the prayer meeting in memory of a Dalit boy *Chakrayaya* from Andhra who used to live in his *Ashram* for a long time. Gandhi said that he would have proposed his name for the top post had he been alive. Four days later, he revealed his heart's desire when Dr. Rajendra Prasad met him.

Gandhi Ji did not stop there. He told it to whomever he met. On 27th June 1947, Gandhi Ji declared in a public gathering, "If I have my way, the President of the Indian Republic will be a chaste and brave Bhangi [sweeper] girl. If an English girl of 17 could become the British Queen and later even Empress of India, there is no reason why a Bhangi girl of robust love of her people and unimpeachable integrity of character should not become the first President of the Indian Republic."[47]

Gandhi wanted to "show to the world that in India there is no one high and no one low." He further said, "If such a girl of my dreams becomes President, I shall be her servant and I shall not expect from the government even my upkeep. I shall make Jawahar Lal, Sardar Patel, and Rajendra Babu her ministers and, therefore her servants."[48]

However, Gandhi's dream remained a dream. It was too radical to realise. The book "*Why Gandhi Still matters: An appraisal for Mahatma's legacy*" (2017) by the Mahatma's grandson and award-winning writer and scholar Rajmohan Gandhi, appraises Gandhi and his legacy by examining some of his most famous (and often most controversial) ideas, beliefs, actions, successes and failures. He quotes Gandhi and tells us in detail, "She should be chaste as Sita and her eyes should radiate light. We shall all salute her and set a new example before the world." The Mahatma was of the view that the election of a Dalit girl would have shown to the world that in India, there is no one high and no one low.

What none of Gandhi's four sons and four daughters-in-law, the fifteen grandchildren and more numerous great-grandchildren could do, another son of the soil, the Gujarati Manus Narendra Modi, did. He declared on 21-6-2022 at exactly 9.52 P.M. in the form of a tweet that the daughter of an adivasi would be the president.

Not only Gandhi but Jaipal Singh Munda also favoured and spoke of more tribal and women representation. I have to tell you and if you have forgotten, I have to remind you that Jaipal Singh Munda (1903-1970) was an Indian politician, writer, and sportsman. He was a member of the Constituent Assembly which debated on the new Constitution of the Indian Union. He captained the Indian field hockey team to clinch gold in the 1928 Summer Olympics. Singh was a gifted speaker and represented all the tribal people of India at the Constituent Assembly of India (which was responsible for drafting the constitution of Independent India). The following is an excerpt from a famous speech made by him on December 19, 1946, where, while welcoming the Objectives Resolution, he highlighted the issues faced by the Indian tribal community:

> As an Adibasi, I am not expected to understand the legal intricacies of the Resolution. But my common sense tells me that every one of us should march in that

road to freedom and fight together. Sir, if there is any group of Indian people that has been shabbily treated, it is my people. They have been disgracefully treated and neglected for the last 6,000 years. The history of the Indus Valley civilization, a child of which I am, shows quite clearly that it is the newcomers — most of you here are intruders as far as I am concerned — it is the newcomers who have driven away my people from the Indus Valley to the jungle fastness ... The whole history of my people is one of continuous exploitation and dispossession by the non-aboriginals of India punctuated by rebellions and disorder, and yet I take Pandit Jawahar Lal Nehru at his word. I take you all at your word that now we are going to start a new chapter, a new chapter of independent India where there is equality of opportunity, where no one would be neglected.[49]

He continued

> "It is only a matter of political window-dressing that today we find six tribal members in this constituent assembly. How is it? ...Is there going to be any provision in the rules whereby it may be possible to bring in more adivasis, and by adivasis **I mean not only men but women also? There are too many men...we want more women.**"[50]

Mrs Murmu's election is a sort of realization of Jaipal Munda's twin wishes – of more tribal and women representation. Gandhi and Munda both must have been celebrating her victory. Though a tribal man belonging to the Garo tribe named P.A. Sangama could not succeed in 2012, yet an attempt was made. In 2012 also BJP backed the tribal and after a decade the party backed a tribal woman, yet this time the BJP was in a comfortable place to sail her through.

PM Modi tweeted that the former Jharkhand governor's understanding of policy matters and compassionate nature will greatly benefit the country. "Smt Droupadi Murmu Ji has devoted her life to serving society and empowering the poor, oppressed as well as the marginalised. She has rich administrative experience and has an outstanding gubernatorial tenure. I am confident she will be a great President of our nation."

PM Narendra Modi saw in her a reflection of himself. She is like him in more ways than one. She does not come from a political background, has no lineage, and had a lifetime of personal struggle and sacrifice. No Harvard but persistent hard work.

As soon as the news of Smt. Droupadi Murmu's nomination flashed, the print and electronic media started telling the audience about her. It was natural. Her first name and her surname both arrest our attention. I can't recollect any other lady who has got this name. Even the spelling of her name was not uniformly written by others. Some write 'Dropadi', others write 'Draupadi'. What is the accepted spelling? Who is "Murmu'? This surname is also not common, though I came across some VIPs who carry this surname.

On June 21, 2022, BJP president J.P. Nadda announced Murmu's candidature, stating that she was chosen out of 20 names after much deliberation amongst the party's Parliamentary Committee. It was said that other than Murmu, the party had considered senior leaders such as current

Vice-President Venkaiah Naidu; governor of Chhattisgarh, Anusuiya Uikey; Governor of Haryana, Bandaru Dattatreya; and Governor of Telangana and Lieutenant Governor of Puducherry, Tamilisai Soundararajan as its presidential candidate. Smt Murmu has been found to be the most suitable candidate among the twenty politicians and intellectuals as she is from the eastern part of India. She is a woman. She is from the Adivasi community. An Adivasi has never had a representative to occupy the highest post in the country. This is what the BJP President Shri Jagat Prakash Nadda said about the President-nominee of India, "it was felt that the new President of India should hail from the East, should be a woman and also belong to the Adivasi community (Ms Murmu belongs to the Santhal community), which has never had a president elected from its community. Looking at all this, it was decided that former Jharkhand Governor, Droupadi Murmu, would be the NDA's candidate for president of India." It is aptly said by Aravindan Neelakandan that 'for building the temple of national development and to make it a model for the whole world, we need the values and guidance of traditional tribal communities.'[51]

Her nomination is 'a reflection of the unwavering resolve of Prime Minister Narendra Modi towards the welfare of women and tribals.' Amit Shah echoed in a familiar and faithful tone. Similarly, other senior leaders said in unison, "There are many reasons for the party cadre to laud this decision. She is a woman, tribal, grounded and humble leader, and hardcore BJP worker and the selection goes well with the BJP's core governance theme -- *Sabka Saath Sabka Vikas, Sabka Vishwas, Sabka Prayas.*

Droupadi Murmu will bring her rich administrative experience, from the district level to state level, also to Rashtrapati Bhavan."

Who is she? Who is Mrs Murmu? Who is Mrs. Droupadi Murmu? You will hardly get any information about her elsewhere. Wikipedia has just a few lines. Google is waiting for more content. Her name is her identity. On 21st June 2022, Yashwant Sinha of AITC was unanimously chosen as the common candidate of UPA and other opposition parties for the 2022 Presidential Election. On the same day, the NDA chose Droupadi Murmu as its presidential candidate. She was chosen from a list consisting of 20 hopefuls. She is a proud member of a Scheduled Tribe. Her tribal identity is being underlined by one and all. She is the first president of India from a tribal community in Odisha.

She is a former governor of Jharkhand and a former Odisha minister. As governor, she made her mark and was known for her sobriety and simplicity and was popular for her accessibility. She is the first tribal President of India and the country's second female President, the first being Pratibha Devi Singh Patil from Maharashtra.

Mrs Murmu continues to break barriers. She is the first president born after India got her freedom from the British-yolk. She was born in 1958 and is even so many years younger to me.

Her name is a message to all. The President of India can be from the most underprivileged community too. There is space at the top for them too. Even the vociferous critics of the BJP couldn't help saying, "with the name of a woman from a tribal community for president, BJP will be giving out the message of having given space to one of the least politically addressed communities. This is something that BJP had time and again been targeted by the opposition for not doing."[52]

Of the 15 presidents the country has seen so far, only six of them came from the south of India. Two of them – Neelam Sanjiva Reddy (1977-82) and V.V. Giri (1969-74) – hailed from Telugu states. Sarvepalli Radhakrishnan, who served as the second president (1962-67), was born in Tamil Nadu's Tiruttani. Yet, Radhakrishnan was a Telugu man. Among former presidents, only V V Giri (1969- 1974) had an Odisha connection. He was born in Berhampur though he was a Telugu from Andhra Pradesh. Therefore it is a proud moment for the people of Odisha that they get their person nominated for the highest office and position of the land.

I think since India has had a Tamil Muslim President in A.P.J. Abdul Kalam; a woman President in Pratibha Patil; and former President Ram Nath Kovind, who belongs to the Scheduled Caste (SC) category, electing a female ST candidate would be the ideal move for the BJP. Ms Murmu was a strong contender for the post before the 2017 presidential elections. But on the occasion, then Bihar Governor Ram Nath Kovind, who happened to be a Dalit, was named as the government's choice for the post. This is also to be noted that "with the elevation of Droupadi Murmu, not only her political and administerial credentials have been credited, but her humble background of starting from a tribal family in Odisha has also been acknowledged."[53]

People who matter and are considered the voice of the intelligentsia tweeted and commented in favour of her nomination. The talk-show debaters debated and registered their views. Rajat Sharma, India TV famed anchor and a distinguished journalist and TV presenter, is overwhelmed with emotions when he comments on her nomination. 'Those who live in the hut never dream of living in Rashtrapati Bhavan. The tribal teacher of the village school, even in the dream, far from becoming the President, will never be able to meet the President in life, does not even think so much. Narendra Modi has encouraged the poor by giving Draupadi Murmu the highest honour." Anand Ranganathan, a Columnist, wrote with pride, "The BJP presidential nominee is a self-made tribal school teacher who rose from abject poverty to great heights and became a two-time legislator and subsequently a governor. The Congress presidential nominee is a man who derisively called Dr. Manmohan Singh a eunuch."

Critics tried to find fault. Some called the move a 'token representation', and Congress' Puducherry handle went further to call Draupadi Murmu a 'dummy'. Chandrasekhar Kalkura felt, "Venkaiah Naidu, with his exemplary track record as one of the best parliamentarians and oratorical skills in multiple languages in Telugu, Kannada, Tamil, English and Hindi, would have been a good choice to be the next president of India."[54]

Vanvasi and tribals liked it. Let me request you to read the following congratulatory message from Vanavasi Kalyan Ashram. ABVKA president Ramchandra Kharadi at the Kendriya Karyakari Mandal meeting held at Namsai in Arunachal Pradesh, issued the statement.

> We recognize this as a historic moment of far-reaching impressions pertaining to the 12-crore Janajati people

of Bharat. The Janajatis are an integral constituent of tradition and inheritors of an esteemed culture of the great Indian nation. However, they have been overlooked and disregarded for many centuries. The ABVKA congratulates Prime Minister Narendra Modi and all the political parties of NDA for nominating a representative of Janajatis for the top most constitutional post in the country.[55]

Master-stroke?

In the words of Dr AK Verma, Political Analyst and Centre for the Study of Society and Politics, the decline of Congress and the increasing support base of the BJP is a sign of how a national party is getting away from the people due to wrong ideology, policies and leadership. Whereas BJP is busy in increasing its base. It may be important to grab power again and again, but even more important is to increase the mass base, and the BJP is doing this very well.

All the presidents (First Citizens of India) BJP chose were from diverse backgrounds. It is BJP that gives proper thought and then decides on a Muslim, a Dalit and now a tribal woman as the president because they are all Rashtravadis. People are amazed and the intellectuals are debating the BJP's game-plan in sending the right person to the Rashtrapati Bhavan whenever they get a chance. They got the opportunity only three times and each time they played a political master-stroke. When this opportunity came up for the first time in 2002, Dr APJ had been picked up. In 2017, Dalit Ram Nath Kovind was elected. Now in 2022, they have given the candidature to a tribal woman. Who can dare say that BJP is anti-Dalit, anti-Muslim or anti-tribals?

In Bikram Vohra's opinion, she is the President for the right reasons and her nomination should not be interpreted as a BJP masterstroke to pull in tribal votes. It is because by using her tribal bloodline as the x-factor, we are only neglecting her 30-year-long service to her country. It is also a disservice to the career graph and abilities of former Governor Murmu that she should be seen as a pawn in a political chess move and not as a person in her own right whose achievements speak for themselves. And they speak eloquently.[56]

Let the debate continue. But one thing is certain. She has fulfilled the wishes of not only Gandhi and his ilk but also of the common tumult of India's countless subalterns. Can they speak? Do they have a voice? The answer is in the affirmative. Anand Vardhan has very deftly concluded his open-minded discussion "Why Droupadi Murmu ticks all boxes for BJP", underlining the significance and importance of such a move as this one.

> Even if the subtext of the BJP's decision to field Droupadi Murmu is in line with the party's symbolic outreach for a wider social base, the new entrant to Rashtrapati Bhavan could hold high symbolic value for the tribal communities and the millions constituting them. In the event of her highly probable election, she could be expected to blend the inherent democratic temper of Indian tribes with the modern values of constitutional statesmanship that befits the highest office of the republic.[57]

Murmu represents a section of our marginalized society. It is the section of the majority of India's rural, agrarian, economically and socially underprivileged. It is the same section that Prime Minister Narendra Modi represents. He too was mocked at by some Lutyens' intellectuals as *"Chaiwala"*. But both Murmu and Modi represent the true India-Marx's proletariat and Socrates' philosopher rolled into one. Indeed as K. R. Narayanan rose by the dint of his hard work, Kovind reached by his perseverance, and Murmu too because of her modest qualities and personal identity. The nation gives everyone of us a chance to reach and touch the sky. It is neither "ism" nor "nobility" that decides. It is the character, passion, service and devotion that pay.

What can I give?

O my fellow citizens!

In giving you receive happiness In body and soul

You have everything to give.

If you have knowledge, share it.

If you have resources,

Share them with the needy Use your mind and heart

To remove the pain of the suffering

And cheer the sad hearts

In giving you receive happiness

Almighty will bless all your actions.

Dr A. P. J. Abdul Kalam, our former President, wrote these lines to underline the contribution of those who enjoy giving to the society. Ms Droupadi Murmu is one such person who has been giving to spread happiness and joy.

Long ago, when Babu Rajendra Prasad, our first President, wrote his autobiography and it was published with a foreword by Sardar Patel, the readers were asked to read it to get inspired to make their lives better and the writer himself said that the readers would like it or not depended on them (*Pathak ise pasand karenge ya nahin yah vahi janen*). It is also noteworthy that the introduction was written on 8th January 1947 and publication of the book was also done in the same month of January 1947 when he was not the President and India was under the British yolk.

In his autobiography, the amity between the two religious communities was cherished and the village life was portrayed in such a way that their brotherhood was on every page of the book.

The Humane President

That is why I am tempted to give her a sobriquet too: "The Humane President". The integral humanist component is in her upbringing. Above all, she is a good human being. When I say "good", I say it with utmost reverence and in all sincerity with all the meanings and connotations attached with the word. Only a good human being can be a good teacher or a good administrator or a good politician. Her greatness lies in her benevolence towards the wretched of the Earth, the marginalised and oppressed. Her humanism is embedded in her personality in such a way that you feel it every time you listen to her. Her simplicity is well known and with her humaneness, warmth and generosity, she is the Humane President. Hers is a long walk in the service of the people. On 25th of July 2022, this name got an additional prefix: Hon'ble President (*Rashtrapati Mahodaya* in Hindi). Her nomination, victory and the oath-taking ceremony is a picture-perfect representation of the aspirations of the people of India. She is going to play an important role of safeguarding the spirit of the constitution and the foundations of our parliamentary democracy. A staunch nationalist, an inspiring speaker, a matchless motivator and a humane soul who believes in leading by example comes from a modest background. She educated herself by working hard to rise against all odds. Her story is the story of all those who have been toiling hard to weave a success story on their own.

When I write these lines and interact with people around me, they seem to suggest that the news of Droupadi Murmu as the 15th President of India is not an ordinary one. It is the victory of all of them who live similar life. People living in villages and small towns, people of all castes and creeds who make both ends meet in the hope of their children getting a good education and coming up in life. The joint family system in which the identity of a person is closely related with the identity of the family and village-like an extended family.

The common man is a winner when the daughter of a tribal villager becomes the President of India. Droupadi Murmu thus becomes a symbol of achievement. Her achievement directs us to fight poverty with hard work, education, clear goals and sustained efforts. She does not belong to the leisure class. She belongs to the labour class.

When India became free in 1947, the young generation had plenty of role models to follow. The Mahatma, Pt Nehru, Sardar Patel and several other leaders inspired them to struggle and be free from poverty and deprivation. Moreover, the youth of that time realised that education could be a strong tool to get rid of a number of impediments in the path of progress.

Child Droupadi's village is not a solitary one where talent is nurtured. In a way, her story is the story of everyone. Those who are born with no silver spoon in their mouths, those who are born to eat what they themselves grow, and those who have boundless energy and deep faith in their parents and God are all like her. Readers! Read your undocumented life through her. Recollect those days when you were born in a village where there was no road, no electricity and no schools. I am not authorised to write about her. The reminiscences I gathered are not mine. Everyone cherishes one's childhood memories and takes pride in one's struggles and victories. One thinks of one's failures as learning curves and is eager to tell others so that others also follow him to get success. Her life—story is important to you and me because we are basically common folk who get inspired by the true story of the tribulations and triumphs of a tribal girl who faced straitened circumstances during her school days. She made a place in the competitive world of Bhubaneswar and not only graduated with flying colours but also rose to greater heights. The life of Ms Droupadi Murmu retells the story of modern India in which an individual's destiny and the social-matrix are welded together. The society in which we live becomes a part of our persona. She learnt how to face failures and defeats and marched forward. She was fortunate enough that she got proper direction and required help at the appropriate time. She withstood and came out of her personal tragedies and loss. Her destiny took her. For her, the woods were many times dark and deep and she fainted too, gasped a little but ultimately overcame.

Fiction Vs Fact: Draupadi-Dopdi/ Droupadi

Name Dopdi Mejhen, age 27, husband Dulna Majhi (deceased), domicile Cherakhan, Bankrahjarh, information whether dead or alive and/or assistance in arrest, one hundred rupees…an exchange between two medallioned *uniforms*.

In passing, I can't help my temptation to recall a story. An aged professor of English should be excused for this usual temptation.

This story was removed from the syllabus of the Delhi University on August 24, 2021. The Delhi University's academic council decided to drop it from the B.A. (honours) syllabus as Left-Liberals found it unacceptable because they were uncomfortable in teaching it. It is Mahasweta Devi's famous short story, *Draupadi(1978)*, translated into English by Gayatri Chakravorty Spivak.

Spivak points out in her foreword to the story "Draupadi" that the two versions of her name mean that either she cannot pronounce the Sanskrit one or that the tribalised form. Dopdi, is the proper name of the ancient Pandava wife. "Dopadi is on the list of wanted persons, yet her name is not on the list of appropriate names for tribal women."

In a retelling of the powerful eponymous character from the Mahabharata, Mahasweta Devi's Draupadi-or Dopdi as she is called –is a rebel who is cornered by the police trying to put down the forces she represents. "What's this, a tribal called Dopadi?" asks a security personnel, at the beginning of the story. "The list of names I brought has nothing like it! How can anyone have an unlisted name?" The second officer responds: Draupadi Mejhen. Born the year her mother threshed rice at Surja Sahu's at Bakuli. Surja Sahu's wife gave her the name.[58]

Without interfering between two intellectuals Sudipata Datta and Makarand R. Paranjape, let me cite what the latter says.

> What the real, as opposed to fictional, Droupadi confirms is that, contrary to the relentless anti-state and some would say anti-national, propaganda against India in general and BJP in particular, both have consistently demonstrated their commitment to our foundational values as enshrined in the Constitution of India. It seems as if the propagandists, by a peculiar irony of Indian democracy, have been decisively proven wrong.[59]

❐

Chapter Four

The Making of a Grand Narrative

There were three occasions when the NDA could choose Presidential candidates. On all three occasions it was inclusive, respected diversity, chose small town and self made persons. When you are driven by a vision the choice reflects that vision.

—B L Santhosh

Election-Mode

As soon as the Election Commission announced that voting for electing India's next president takes place on 18th July and the counting of votes on 21st July, 2022 everyone concerned got into attention mode. The BJP knew that it had numbers and, along with its allies, they would have an easy majority in the presidential Electoral College. No President, with the exception of first President Rajendra Prasad, has got a second term and it was out of the question to give another five-year term to Shri Ram Nath Kovind. So the party wanted to nominate the best one according to their calculations and understanding, which is often guided by the idea of India put forward by the Rashtravadis.

This is the third time when the BJP chose a president who comes from a humble background and has the image of having given his or her life for the betterment of the community. Droupadi Murmu is the manifestation and embodiment of social justice and women empowerment.

Bommarabettu Laxmijanardhana Santhosh is an Indian politician currently National General Secretary of Bharatiya Janata Party from 15th July 2019. He is the most high-profile General Secretary who commands enormous influence and respect as he is the link between the party and its ideological patron (RSS). When he says that Mrs Murmu's elevation to the post is a rare occasion when crores feel that one amongst us has risen to the top, he means it. He indicates that the party takes the selection of presidential candidates quite seriously. The nomination and election of Murmu sends a strong political signal around the country, especially to the states where the tribal community is in a great number. The ruling BJP under PM Narendra Modi got enough support from this community in the last two general elections, but it was not commendable. It lacked spirit and totality. In 2019, out of 47 reserved seats for MPs, BJP got only 35. In some of the states where the Vanvasi community is in sufficiently large numbers, BJP couldn't form its government at the state level. In Odisha, Jharkhand, and Chhattisgarh, there is still ample scope to grow. Even in Gujarat, the tribal community cannot be left unattended.

Alok Mehta, editorial director of ITV Network India News and Aaj Samaj Dainik, is an experienced editor. He has very skilfully captured the entire landscape and background when he writes. "Narendra Modi has been preparing since the beginning, keeping in mind the far-reaching political and national goals and keeping his intentions very patiently confidential. His footsteps are extremely difficult to predict. Similarly, senior leaders of Rashtriya Swayamsevak Sangh, who support the BJP and select loyal campaigners, are engaged in active service campaigns among people in different states, rural forest dwelling areas, and northeastern states. In a way, they are silently engaged in arranging land, manure, water, and light for the political success of the BJP. Modi's efforts to take his victory chariot to non-BJP ruled states like Odisha, Telangana, Andhra, Kerala, and Tamil Nadu, make new agreements, and make a strong image of India at the international level too to serve political, social, and economic interests, will thus meet with success."[60]

The question "Does Murmu deserve to be India's President merely because she hails from an Adivasi community?" doesn't hold solid grounds as this was not the only factor in her favour when her candidature was being finalised.

Murmu's nomination is a well-thought-out plan by the NDA to showcase how Prime Minister Narendra Modi's government focused on giving representation to the marginalised sections of society. Earlier, President Ram Nath Kovind comes from the Dalit community. Kovind hails from a small Koli community of Uttar Pradesh, born in a farmer's mud house and he became India's second Dalit President. In 2017, Ram Nath Kovind, a Dalit (of Kori-Koli sub-caste or weaver) leader from Uttar Pradesh, became the President of India. As per CSDS-Lokniti post-poll surveys, the number of Jatavs voting for the BJP-led alliance went up to 21 per cent in 2022 from 8 per cent in 2017 and non-Jatavs to 41 per cent from 32 per cent for the same period. It was a significant gain and some credit should have gone to his thoughtful nomination by the party in power. Once it was felt that governance issues notwithstanding, the BJP's arithmetic could not be breached, it was natural to go ahead this time too in the similar way.

A tribal woman succeeding a Dalit to the highest constitutional post of the nation is an outstanding demonstration to the expanding basis of Indian democracy. Droupadi Murmu highlights the priority of the government about giving a fair representation to the people from the underprivileged communities. "Coming back to back to the successful nomination of incumbent President Ram Nath Kovind, a Dalit leader, it must give the two most vulnerable social groups of India — the Scheduled Castes and Scheduled Tribes — an immense emotional satisfaction and an augmented sense of ownership of the country where a son and daughter of their own would head the Republic."[61]

In 2002, the BJP led ruling NDA fielded India's 'Missile Man' Dr APJ. He was a Muslim. This I call, "One Vision Three Occasions: From Kalam to Kovind to Murmu."

Three gains with one action

Arati R Jerath, a Delhi-based senior journalist, writes in an opinion piece that in one stroke, the BJP, as well as PM Narendra Modi, has accomplished three things. One, the choice of an Adivasi woman to occupy the highest office in the country sends a powerful message of social inclusion. Two, he has finessed the opposition with masterful skills. Three, the hope of a political windfall for the BJP as well as the RSS is ensured.

"Mr Modi is essentially a political animal, and he is conscious of the political impact of a potential move. In choosing a presidential candidate, he's also looking for somebody who could potentially help the BJP." Ashok Malik says. Therefore, the candidate who could help the BJP's growth has been an essential part of the entire search-exercise. One who can be an embodiment and representative of inclusiveness and diversity can adorn the place of pride. In other words, Modi wants his party to represent the New India of prosperity, equality and socio-economic mobility, reflecting the true embodiment of samajik samarasta (social harmony)"[62] says Aditi Narayani Paswan.

What is the Vision of Narendra Modi that he wishes to realize? It is to win the hearts and mind of people. The answer to this question is not easy to find. "Modi is a weaver of a complex political fabric which is strong and represents different hues of our political and social spectrum" answers one of Modi's admirers. "Prime Minister Modi doesn't want to merely govern India, he wants to craft a new kind of pluralism which rejects congress' skull-cap secularism" Kaveree Bamzai once commented.

On May 12, 2022, Bharuch Gujarat) was celebrating an "Utkarsh samaroh". It was a part of the celebration in recognition of Shri Narendra Modi's completion of eight years in service as the PM of India. The PM spoke his mind in the virtual rally. This is an extract of the article written by Kamal Saiyed in the Indian Express dated May 13, 2022.

> Modi said, "once I met a leader…he is a very senior leader…he has been a political opponent. But I do respect him. One day, he came to meet me, to sort out some issues. He said, "Modiji, now what else do

you want to do? The country has made you the prime minister twice.

Modi said, "He thought that becoming prime minister twice was a huge achievement.

He does not know that this Modi is made of something else ...It is the soil of Gujarat that has shaped me. It is not enough that I should rest now, (thinking) that everything that has happened is good...no...My dream is saturation...meet your target 100 percent.

Get the government machinery into a habit, create faith in the citizens.[63]

The nomination of Mrs Murmu was a well-thought-out move to continually reach even those who have been unreachable or not fast-paced. When Modi says that her understanding of grassroots problems and vision for India's development is outstanding, his plan too is included in it. Murmu is a grassroots politician. She has many firsts to her credit. She served as a minister and a governor. She was a known person and the leaders at the helm knew her well. She was also considered for the presidential post in 2017. In 2022, the condition was found to be more favourable to her than before. The assembly elections in Gujarat, Madhya Pradesh, Rajasthan, and Chhattisgarh are fast approaching and these four states have 128 seats reserved for Scheduled Tribes of which the BJP had won just 35 seats last time. Therefore, it was thought that her election would be seen by voters with positivity.

Four pillars of Positivity

The choice of Mrs Murmu as the President of India rests on four pillars or premises. To my mind, the criterion of selection was based on these four factors. The person should be inclusive, diverse, from a small town and self-made. A tribal woman leader being in the Rashtrapati Bhavan, the official residence of the President of India, signals both inclusion and diversity.

1. Inclusiveness of all

The quality of including many different types of people and treating them all fairly and equally is called inclusiveness. "Modi has consistently increased the social base of the BJP, making it far more inclusive and, in the process; he has almost totally transformed it compared to the days when it was seen as a party of the urban middle class and trader."[64]

In Modi's vision, India is for all her citizens, not just a privileged few. The privileged were placed in that category through religion, caste, language and wealth. He thinks that our India should be such that every Indian would be proud to own and claim to be his own. He follows the words of Ambedkar, "the most vital need of the day is to create among the mass of people, a sense of common nationality, a feeling not that they are Indians first and Hindus, Mohammedans or Sindhis and Canarese afterwards, but that they are Indians first and Indians last."[65]

Mrs Droupadi Murmu represents such a person who is an epitome of inclusiveness. Indian democracy is considered inclusive in theory but this attempt makes it possible to practically implement the spirit of the constitution. No one should be excluded from the democratic processes and here was a case that a tribal was not able to reach at the highest post. The present-day government made it possible. This is the most ideal kind of situation in which even the most under-privileged also can feel secured and empowered. Droupadi Murmu's elevation and projection are a testament of the government's inclusive politics. "The choice of an Adivasi woman to occupy the highest office in the country sends a powerful message of social inclusion. Almost every important community has been represented in Rashtrapati Bhavan over the past seven decades, except the tribal-community. Murmu's election smashed another glass ceiling in the struggle for the empowerment of marginalised social and gender groups, symbolic though it may be."[66]

'The Hindustan Times' considered opinion is in the following tweet, "Projecting Droupadi Murmu's nomination as the NDA's presidential candidate as a testament of its inclusive politics. The BJP is hopeful that it will consolidate its position." Ms Droupadi Murmu is also of the view that the government should cover all sections of society, including farmers, the poor, the exploited and the deprived. In the rapid path of development, everyone should participate and contribute.

2. Respecting Diversity

It is the firm belief of the party and its leader that "Unity in diversity is the identity of India. The harmonious coexistence of different religions, sections and beliefs in the country is our speciality and for strengthening the socio-cultural fabric of the country in different periods."[67] The choice and nomination of Smt. Droupadi Murmu was to send the message to the entire population of India that they respect diversity and wish the others also that they should also do so. When the opposition has nothing more to offer than Yashwant Sinha, an ex-BJP leader, it was found to be correct to present in her a representative of the Idea of India the party offers and envisages.

3. From small town

Hailing from a backward village in Odisha's Mayurbhanj district, Murmu was found to be the right candidate according to the Criteria fixed. She is from a small town whose population is less than 30000. Harvard is being ignored and hard work is being given the credit; that is why a simple B.A. was considered enough as far as educational qualifications are concerned. Kalam was from a small town, Kovind too was born in a small town, and similarly, Murmu hails from a small town.

4. Self-made person

She is a self-made person, like Modi. She represents the archetypal self-made one who has come up in her life quietly through hard work and selfless service. Since early childhood, she was not ambitious and her dream was also not too big not to be realised. Her desire was just to learn something to earn something and give a part of it to her parents, who were hand to mouth. She took a bold step in her teens and, with firmness and resolve, reached the capital city of her state to learn and earn. In this way, she made herself capable of standing on her own. She not only stood firm on the ground, but she helped others too to come up. When she got to take care of her children also, she didn't keep herself within the four walls of her home. She went out and started teaching in a school without asking for a salary. Whatever honorarium she got, she took it and continued guiding and teaching others, including her own sons and daughter. You will be surprised to know that her teaching was so effortless and effective that her students used to get good marks without going for any private tuition. She won her first political election as a councillor because her parents voted for her trusting her teaching skills. "If she can teach so well, she will administer well too," was the refrain.

Mrs Droupadi Murmu is from a small town and is a self-made person. She fulfils the requirement of diversity and inclusiveness. What else do you want?

If you still have some lingering questions, let me convince you to take the words of BJP national General Secretary C T Ravi, who says that a feeling that the Adivasi woman is not capable of the position itself depicts one's nasty mindset. The mindset of indulging in false propaganda against a self-made Adivasi woman who has proved her capability is dangerous. The state of mind that feels one alone to be worthy is dangerous. Murmu, an Adivasi woman, has already proved her capabilities, as the Governor of Jharkhand, as a minister and MLA in Odisha and as a lecturer in a college. A feeling that the Adivasi woman is not capable of the position itself depicts one's nasty mindset.[67]

Lotus to Potus

I find amazing similarities between Murmu and Harris. Kamala Harris became the Vice President of The US in 2021. Droupadi Murmu became President of India in 2022.

Kamala's name is associated with the 'lotus', and Droupadi's name is associated with the party that has the election symbol 'lotus.' Kamala Harris got her surname from her father; Droupadi Murmu got it from her husband. Kamala lived with the commoners and her family's closest friends were black people. Kamala is the 'Daughter of Oakland", and Droupadi is the "Daughter of Rairangpur." Kamala faced racial discrimination as a child, and Droupadi also found her formative years financially challenging.

We have travelled a lot since then. Mrs Droupadi Murmu is our 1[5th] President. In the US, every aspiring leader writes her biography. In Independent India, they write when they retire. Kamala Harris wrote her biography "The Truth we hold: An American Journey" in 2019. Then she became the Vice President of America. In my book on Kamala Harris, I wrote, "It is the life experience of a woman who failed not once but twice but never gave up. Kamala Harris's personal narrative is not just a story of race or ethnicity or gender; it is an Indian story as well."[69] About Droupadi Murmu, she herself says, "NDA government has now proven BJP's slogan of "Sab Ka Saath, Sab Ka Biswas" by selecting a tribal woman for the top post."

It is heartening to note that Kamala Harris and Droupadi Murmu both represent their respective countries. They are the ideals of inclusiveness and diversity. Both are self-made persons and are from small towns.

If you don't know what 'Potus' is, let me tell you that 'Potus' is the abbreviation for President of the United States.

A dream comes true

It is a fact that Smt Droupadi Murmu never ever nurtured a dream to be the President of India. She was not in a position to even think of governorship. But it happened. Our Former President Ram Nath Kovind went with his wife to Mashobra in Himachal Pradesh to celebrate their 43rd wedding anniversary. During sight-seeing, they wandered into the premises of the Retreat building, the president's summer palace. It is a wonderful world. Those who denied him entry became his most obedient servants. During a casual chat with some of his family members, Pranab Mukherjee, after being administered the oath-of-office as India's 13th president, was asked whether he had ever dreamt of entering the august precincts of the Rashtrapati Bhawan as its foremost occupant. In reply, Mukherjee reportedly said, albeit in a lighter vein, "I had often told myself that being the president is a far cry, but in my next life- if there is one- even if I am born as one of those horses that pull the president's ceremonial carriage to that red-sand-stone palace, it will be an accomplishment of sorts."

This is the magic of our democratic traditions that those, like Droupadi Murmu, who never nurtured the dream of even visiting the place as a tourist get a chance to reside there.

Dreaming Big in New India

There was a time when even the high and mighty could not dream big as the two instances you just read portray. Even the would-be presidents couldn't dream to be presidents. Dr APJ tried to teach us to dream big. But, unfortunately, he died of teaching the next generation and taught us to dream of a 2020 new India. Alas! The new India of 2020 brought a pandemic. But we have learnt a lesson about withstanding pressures. The next generation has already started dreaming big, and in almost all fields, they are achieving big.

Droupadi Murmu, walking side by side with the top most VVIPs of the country, makes a big impact on the minds of youth. The marginalised group takes it as a godsend gift. An enlightened member of such a group, Aditi Narayani Paswan, has this to add to the ongoing discourse. "This has inspired many young women from marginalized communities, like me, to dream big. Droupadi Murmu is not just a source of inspiration for us; her life and struggle, determination, and success in the face of great odds represent the hope and promise of New India."[70]

Hope and promise of a new India is a really big thing which is being offered by these acts of determination and resolve. There is a long way to go.

❐

Chapter Five

Droupadi Murmu's contribution to tribal welfare

Truth be told the tribal belt should be happy for one of their own being elevated and have great expectations that their outstanding social and economic issues will be resolved (and there are many of these) but they do not have to be grateful or unquestioningly surrender their choice of franchise.

—Bikram Vohra

Herself a Tribal

Droupadi Murmu is known to be most expressive on the issues of tribals and their all-round welfare. This is natural also. She is herself a tribal. But there are many who claim that they know better than her. Even Yashwant Sinha said that he had done more than her for the welfare of tribals. It is also not a requirement to be a tribal to work for their welfare. The question is raised because of our high expectations. She has given hope to many tribal organisations and community members of the country that she will protect the interests of about ten percent of the country's population.

Demands and Issues

There are so many demands and expectations. The entire population of STs and even SCs requires various reforms and laws. Tribal people living on the margins for years will be happy with Droupadi Murmu's presidency only when PESA (Panchayat Extension to Schedule Area Act 1996) becomes the way for the law to be empowered. PESA law has been implemented to ensure the rights of the tribals on water, forest, and land, but it did not benefit the tribals much. When the Sarna Dharma Code is included in the Census Form, the coordination of the Central Government with the States of the Fifth and Sixth Schedule can become effective. According to the 2011 census, there are about 12 crore tribal people in the country. They have a strong presence in the fifth and sixth schedule states. If political analysts are to be believed, the candidature of Droupadi Murmu will help the BJP make a dent in the tribal vote in the fifth and sixth schedule states.

The Sixth Schedule States of Assam, Meghalaya, Tripura, and Mizoram have a large number of tribal people. Assam has 12 percent, Tripura 31 percent, Meghalaya 86 percent, and Mizoram has more than 95 percent of people in this community. On the other hand, Jharkhand has about 27 percent tribals in the fifth schedule states. Chhattisgarh has 30, Madhya Pradesh 21, Odisha 22.85, Rajasthan 13.48, Gujarat 8, West Bengal 5.8, Rajasthan 13.48, and Himachal Pradesh 5.7 percent population. Therefore, BJP's eyes are on Odisha, Rajasthan, Jharkhand, and Chhattisgarh.

The BJP is being challenged by regional parties in the fifth and sixth schedule states in the country. BJP is keen to connect tribal society to defeat YSRC in Andhra Pradesh, JMM in Jharkhand, Biju Janata Dal in Odisha, and Trinamool Congress in West Bengal.

Expectations and Limits

Her Excellency Droupadi Murmu is now the President of India. This in itself is a very important beginning. She comes from the tribal community and the tribal community has a lot of expectations from her. The debates and dialogues that started with her nomination have helped bring tribal issues into the limelight. And it's going to be beneficial to the community in the near future.

Why would the tribals not want Murmu to use the influence of her position for the development and progress of their society? There are many problems and many solutions. Many tribal people of the country get angry on hearing this that they have started being called 'Vanwasi'. This is exactly like Gandhiji's suggestion of calling 'Dalit' as 'Harijan'. But the people who address them as Vanwasi also want the welfare of the tribals. They also want the tribal people to remain a part of the Sanatan form of Hinduism. Many people oppose this too. They believe they do not have the same relationship with Hinduism as they are told. They are nature lovers, and if they have any religion, then it is 'Sarna' which should be recognized now. Followers of this faith do not believe in idol worship and instead respect the forces of nature, be it forests, hills, rivers, or land. In the absence of a Sarna code, adherents enlist themselves in the category "Other Religions and Persuasion (ORP)" during the census exercise. There is concern about losing identity, culture, and traditional way of life without formal recognition. Most of the tribals want to avoid falling prey to attempts to convert to Hinduism and Christianity.

This is considered against the ideological framework of the Rashtriya Swayamsevak Sangh (RSS) and its agenda of incorporating tribals within the larger Hindu identity. Tribal community leaders and parties, including the Jharkhand Mukti Morcha (JMM), have been advocating the need for a separate code for Sarna religion during the next census. On the other hand, the conversion of India's tribes to Christianity and the change in demography is a big blow to the country. This has been a big issue. Over the years, north-eastern states such as Nagaland, Mizoram, and Meghalaya have become Christian-dominated. There is a fear that the conversion will have an impact on the rest of India. Christian missionaries started working here in the early 19th century. Despite this, it has very little presence in states like Jharkhand, Odisha, Chhattisgarh, and West Bengal. These states have a large tribal population. Jharkhand has the highest Christian population (only 4.3%) among these states as per the last census. Various organisations like Vanwasi Kalyan Ashram have been trying to do tribal welfare work like Christian missionaries. According to Professor Badri Narayan, "tribal deities are placed inside Hindu temples" to "create a Hindu-tribal synergy" in these areas. The plan to keep tribal society away from Christianity and assimilate them into Hinduism has also had an effect.

Droupadi Murmu has been nominated by the Prime Minister and his party and this is part of his plan in which he is, on the one hand, orienting the Pasmanda group of the Muslim community to the Bharatiya Janata Party. On the other hand, he is also targeting the tribal groups settled in many states of India. By making aware, running a campaign to connect with the mainstream of politics and society, should also be seen from the point of view of the growing consciousness of the social concerns of the Bharatiya Janata Party. Over the years, the tribal society of the Hindu population has been looked upon by foreign missionaries. Since most of these people are naive and mainly worship nature in the name of religion, they are first motivated to separate their own religion from Sanatan Dharma. Then gradually, they are initiated into their religion. It is also ensured that they continue to get the benefit of reservations fixed for Scheduled Tribes. For this, a lot of money comes from abroad. Although Santhal means a calm person, they also know how to sacrifice everything for their pride, fame, and glory. There was a fight for independence in 1857, but these tribal people started challenging the East India Company of the British many years before this. These people were neglected for a long time. Now a new spark of consciousness will come among them from the election of Droupadi Murmu and it is hoped that it will be fruitful.

One of the many decisions of the National Executive of the BJP in Hyderabad was to organise several meetings and events in the tribal areas of the country with the official portrait of the President of Droupadi Murmu to inform that a well-educated and conscious woman from among them is now the supreme leader of the country. She has got the highest post. She is the President of the Republic of India. It will have many benefits. The immediate benefit would be that the BJP would get an electoral edge. A total of 128 seats are reserved for Scheduled Tribes (STs) in four electoral states - 27 in Gujarat, 25 in Rajasthan, 29 in Chhattisgarh, and 47 in Madhya Pradesh. In the last assembly elections, BJP could win only 35 of these seats. The BJP is already gearing up for next year's Rajasthan assembly elections and is eyeing around 70 seats through Murmu, which has a sizable tribal population. Although 25 seats are reserved for STs, the community's influence can be seen around 70 seats. According to the 2011 census, the tribal community constitutes about 14 percent of the population of Rajasthan. That is why the five MLAs of Rajasthan who were included as proponents of Murmu were tribals. Through them, the BJP is hoping to reach the tribal vote-bank in these 70 seats. After Murmu ji becomes the President, rallies will be organised in all the villages. Organisers have been asked to use the official photograph of the President that will be released after he is elected. All villages and gram panchayats will be involved in these rallies. BJP will try to connect all the tribal people and leaders with the mainstream of the country and their party through these rallies.

In a way, Hindu revival led to many 'subaltern' communities, hitherto outside the BJP fold, started coming closer to the party and showed not only their interest but also willingness to follow suit. This is not the only motive behind giving a person of tribal society a position called symbolic by some scholars. This would be a betrayal for the tribal society. In fact, the country is now taking a step in the direction that 'Sabka Sath' is now completely 'Sab's'. It was not just a slogan; it was not a mere promise. Her arrival at Rashtrapati Bhavan is the beginning of a worldwide revolution. It has been the project of many people sitting in India that tribals and Dalits should be separated from Hinduism. They do this work with foreign financial help. Now the government does not want this to happen. Those who take political advantage of the so-called social activities being done with foreign funding or foreign aid for religious conversion and forced conversion will be cracked down. By connecting and keeping the tribals in the mainstream will and will gain momentum like a movement with the election of President Murmu.

We must remember that Droupadi Murmu's thirty years of commitment and service towards her people have rewarded her on the one hand. On the other hand, she is also becoming a powerful medium for their upliftment. One in eleven Indians of the country comes from tribal society, so when they see that one of them is sitting in the highest office of the country, then they will surely feel proud. Being happy with this decision, many will also give their vote to BJP in the upcoming elections. The self-respecting community, which has never learned to bow down, will automatically know the meaning and implication of the dignity of the presidency of the country.

Language Issues and Matters

Santal is an English form adopted from Hindi which corresponds with the form Saontar used by Bengali-speaking people of Bengal. Most anthropologists agree that Santal is a name given to them by non-Santals. In fact, Santals among themselves use the term HOR, meaning man (human). Some living in Bengal and Orrisa use the term Manjhi to designate their identity. They had no written history until the British colonialists and western missionaries came to India in the 18th century. Before that, they passed on their history, customs and traditions orally through their stories, songs, and legends, as they did not have their own script. But they have kept their language SANTALI alive even to the present day, which is one of the sources of tracing their origin, migration, history and glories.[71]

Murmu also called for the translation of published literature on tribal languages and culture. She has always praised the contribution of great personalities like Lako Bodra and Raghunath Murmu. It also said that the regulators of the 'Varanchiti script' of 'Ho' tribes and 'Ol Chiki' script of Santhali should be given due respect. She has been of the view that tribal history is not well presented and needs to be "re- established" and 'rewritten'.

To conclude, one can join with Ram Madhav, who has very adroitly suggested that the real success of our democracy is when President Murmu is looked at as not merely a 'tribal President' but the President of the 1.3 billion people—strong- Republic of India. For her election to symbolize the bridging of the gap between the first and last citizens of our republic, people should celebrate the occasion by installing her picture in every public space. The 'murti' jibe of an inexperienced political novice has turned on him. Now that Droupadi Murmu is the President of the Republic of India, her picture will be displayed in every nook and corner.

It will be an exercise in futility to pre-judge Droupadi Murmu at this stage. As the president of our great nation, she will receive unabiding love and respect due for the office of the president. The constitution of India will be there to guide her. She is the glory of the republic. She is the honour of the nation. She is Pradhan Sevak and the very first in all respects.

❐

Chapter Six

Droupadi Murmu: Beyond Symbolism and Tokenism

People elect their representatives from the Gram Panchayat to Parliament. They vest their will and hopes in these representatives. In turn, the people's representatives devote their lives to the service of the nation. But our endeavours are not for ourselves alone.[72]

—Ram Nath Kovind

A Symbolic head?

When former President Ram Nath Kovind spoke these words, he was not aware that the words he was speaking were going to be a soothsayer's words. In Droupadi Murmu, we find a representative who started serving the masses from the gram panchayat level and reached the top. Her service to the nation till date has been exemplary and the reward of her service is also breathtaking.

She represents us, the common people like you and me. We are the majority of India, agrarian, rural, socially, and economically underprivileged. She is one among us. The commoners think and wish that she will empathise with them as she knows their plight. The fact that a woman belonging to a tribal community was elected illustrates how the common man identifies with her. This is a big step for India.

She belongs to a community. She is a tribal. This has been highlighted by almost everyone who writes about her. There is no doubt that her nomination was based on several factors and this one was one of the major factors. Another factor is that her stint as a governor of Jharkhand was noteworthy and successful. She was called a governor of great integrity and honesty. Whatever she could, she did very efficiently. Her relationship with the Chief Ministers remained cordial and good.

These are some of the attributes that helped her to become a person who created history and it is up to her now to prove her critics wrong. Tribals will also get a kind of social and economic transformation when they see a tribal as the President of their country.

They will change as nothing can inspire more than a symbolic head. The flag, the emblem, and the anthem all inspire. People die for the protection of a mere flag. The president is also a figurehead. President Droupadi Murmu is a signifier of her tribal identity too. It goes without saying that signs and symbols can be used to tell a lie too. All signifiers, says Derrida, and the first and foremost the written signifier, are derivative with regard to what would wed the voice indissolubly to the mind. That is why her elevation is neither 'hollow symbolism' nor 'tokenism'. Her election is momentous. We need to go beyond the symbolism and cynicism that has dominated the narrative. It is good fortune for the tribal population in the country. It is a victory of tribal political ambitions and a step forward in the right direction for the community.

Against Tokenism and symbolism

The Indian president is a mere figurehead who, in the words of former Prime Minister Jawaharlal Nehru, is a 'head that neither reigns nor governs' and holds a position of 'authority or dignity' more than anything else? The election of Droupadi Murmu as the republic's president reignited the debate. A question is being asked and asked forcefully, "Is the role of the nominal head of India the most judicious place for gender, geographical and communal tokenism?

The opposition parties were of the view that NDA's decision to nominate Murmu, a tribal candidate, for the presidential election was mere 'tokenism'. KTR from Telangana said, "We don't believe in tokenism. It is not about Murmu's candidature. She represents a party which is heavily reliant on unconstitutional practices."[73] They are of the view that the plight of Dalits has not changed much after Ram Nath Kovind, a member of the community, became the President. They have been repeatedly saying that BJP has not done anything for the welfare of the tribal community in the last eight years. Speaking about Murmu's candidature, KTR said, "Bhishma was defeated since he was on Kauravas' side in Mahabharat. Tokenism for tribal people in the form of Droupadi Murmu is not correct. She was a minister when 13 tribal people were killed in a steel plant agitation in Kalianganagar of Odisha in 2006. She has not condemned it."[74]

The opposition was of the view that by nominating Droupadi Murmu as the Presidential candidate, the BJP has tried to play the politics of tokenism. They settled for a person who is a tribal in name and Hindu nationalist in ideology. The move will not be able to assuage the feelings of the tribal community as they often feel left out. There is an element of truth in the saying that they will not change as a tribal is a president. No one can disagree when Vivek Deshpande says that there is no guarantee that a community will actually benefit by having a person from its ranks at the helm. "Consider the example of the late activist Brahmadev Sharma who worked relentlessly for the justice of tribals and pioneered the Panchayat Raj (extension to Scheduled Areas) Act, 1996. The law resulted in the single biggest boost to the cause of Adivasi empowerment and justice in the history of independent India. Sharma was, by birth, a Brahmin."[75]

For Tokenism and Symbolism

The tribal society had suffered neglect for years despite being an integral part of Indian tradition and culture. In the words of Mohan Guruswami, "like indigenous people all over the world, India's adivasis too have been savaged and ravaged by later people claiming to be more "civilised". They are now easily its most deprived and oppressed section. There have been many supporters in the intellectual circle and common people who have been saying that in the real world, even tokenism and symbolism is an essential tool for social upliftment and emancipation. BJP national General Secretary C T Ravi has termed this kind of adverse thinking of the opposition as the result of a 'nasty mindset."

Symbolism has always been of great importance in politics. The importance of symbols is so much that even the chosen symbol of a party becomes a symbol. In the beginning, when India got her independence and the first general elections were announced, the Congress party kept a pair of two bullocks as election symbols to woo the farmers. If Jana Sangh's 'Deepak' was a symbol of light, then BJP's 'Lotus' is also a symbol. BJP MP Vijay Kumar Malhotra had even written a book to explain the 'lotus' symbol.

Today, due to Bahin Mayawati, Kanshi Ram etc., respect has also increased among Dalits. When Bahin Ji can become chief minister then anything can happen. She had started installing her idols by making her election symbol a symbol. Through symbols, a sense of confidence and respect in an understanding is awakened. It also leads to mutual bonding. On the one hand, they get attached to each other; secondly, they start having a good feeling towards other communities also. Those feelings and these thoughts bring unity to the entire society and country. When the Prime Minister of India and the members of his cabinet support the appointment of a person who has not been represented before, respect and trust increases for such people. With Droupadi Murmu's name being proposed and her becoming the President of the country, there was no indicative initiative; a message was sent that the country was ready to do everything to bring tribal society into the mainstream. The highest office of the country like that of the President can be offered to a tribal woman, which no one can even dream of. From a political point of view, this move can be considered as a paradigm-changing one. This is the result of giving wings to the aspirations of the people. It is not only atonement for the neglect being done towards them for ages; it is also repentance. Whether it is the selection of Ram Nath Kovind and whether it is now Murmu, every time society has got the mantra of goodwill through them. This is: *sabka saath sabka vikas*.

Those who advocate following the middle path say that "symbolism can't be ignored because it marks a major step towards making politics inclusive and achieving social justice. It forces other political parties to recalibrate their stand and shakes politics out of its slumber. It also pushes political analysts to search for a new lens to view the party they believe is avowedly 'upper caste'.[76]

Murmu being in such a high position is not just a synonym for 'political symbolism' to benefit her caste etc. But there is a lesson which can be of great benefit if one takes it in a positive way and considers that incumbent person as his ideal. For example, after Dr Kalam became the President, the Muslims did not have any extra respect nor did their respect and place in the society increase. People still don't see Kalam as a Muslim alone. He was considered the 'People's President'. The youth considered him as their role model. He has been a youth Icon. They appreciate the books written by him. The best seller of his autobiography is still maintained by the youth. He was 'Ajatshatru'. What a grand thing! Not only is this, the party that proposed his name still feels proud of him.

Though it is out of place to discuss the case of Mayawati, yet you can yourself see that she didn't do much for the caste she belonged to. She was both a woman and a leader from a Scheduled Caste and was able to win elections but was not able to bring drastic changes in the lives of the people she represented. She was considered the Prime Minister of the future as she played an important role in the party politics of the state of UP but failed miserably. Post-2014 elections, she is also considered to run. The BSP supremo Mayawati's support for Murmu was keeping in mind that the Adivasi samaj is an important part of the party's movement.

Think about Obama. Electing a black President was a great tokenism. He also didn't bring about any radical change in the lives of the black people. The still shout, 'black lives matter.' The deep-rooted racism in the American society is still there. Mr Obama won and the USA could say with pride that they can elect a black man as their President. Similar is the case of Kamala Harris. The Republicans who opposed his candidature for ideological and political reasons ended up looking low and subdued. Therefore, electing Droupadi Murmu, who is a tribal woman, will be more than a tokenism. It will create a kind of social movement. Her momentous victory makes the ideological and political claims of the opposition party feeble and weak.

Supporting a tribal woman can be criticised as tokenism, but then it is not the first time tokenism has affected presidential polls. In 2007, for instance, the Congress selected Pratibha Patil, who was not a political heavyweight or household name. There were times when the claim of Jagjeevan Ram was ignored and even the talk of tokenism was kept aside then. He happened to be from the Scheduled Castes. His daughter Meira Kumar was defeated by another Dalit in the last presidential election. All these incidents indicate that the political narratives are formed keeping in mind so many factors and different kinds of excuses and arguments are offered for or against the decisions taken by the party-bigwigs.

On the other hand, political leaders belonging to tribal communities say that it is a proud movement for Adivasis, who are the original inhabitants of the county. It has a civilizational importance. Arjun Munda, the three-term chief minister of Jharkhand, said,

> Her nomination should not be seen as tokenism or an ornamental decision by the BJP. The Adivasis have not migrated to India. They are the sons and daughters of the soil. It has a larger implication for Indian policy. "Earlier, everybody got an opportunity to tell (the tribals how to improve). Now, for the first time, an "original inhabitant' has got an opportunity to listen and play the role of a constitutional head of the country (Abhi tak sabko kahney ka mauka mila hai, pahli baar sunane ka mauka diya hai ," This is unprecedented.[77]

Leaving aside the symbolic importance of a leader making it to Rashtrapati Bhavan from the most underprivileged of social strata or succumbing to a temptation to overstate its inspirational value to a larger demographic group sharing the identity, one must simply appreciate that for once, a tribal leader, representing a large number of people, no longer needs to see even the position of the First Citizen of the country as a glass ceiling.[78]

Not an empty symbolic gesture

"The election of Murmu cannot be an empty symbolic gesture, mere lip service to inclusion. It must signal a new era where it cannot continue to be business as usual, where entitlements and allotments can no longer be so routinely denied. Murmu's presence as head of State, albeit without real political power, must signal a new morality where there are renewed efforts to right a historical wrong; to improve the lives of 43.8% of tribals who live below the poverty line; to improve infant and maternal mortality; to bridge the education gap."[79] Namita Bhandare writes emphatically. Ritambhara Hebbar, a professor at the Centre for Study of Developing Societies of the Mumbai-based Tata Institute of Social Sciences, told DW, "I would not call her nomination as symbolic. It is a fight for political legitimacy in the mainstream and the national political system. Her rise epitomises a struggle, and she has worked her way up — a reflection of her political acuteness."

My Tribal Vs Your Tribal

Gargi Verma of Indian Express has very adroitly written about the Murmu conundrum among the tribal MP and MLA who do not belong to the NDA. They found it hard to find the way out. They could not ignore the candidature of a tribal candidate for the post of the President of India, but the Congress government in tribal-dominated Chhattisgarh had found a lame excuse. CM Bhupesh Baghel raised the case of another tribal leader. She is Anusuiya Uikey. She is also a tribal leader, but her party is used by Congress. She is the governor of Chhattisgarh. Uikey has been an MLA from the assembly constituency Damua from 1985 to 1990. She was also the Minister of the Women and Child Development Department from 1988 to 1989 in the Arjun Singh Government of Madhya Pradesh. However, he later left Congress. After joining the BJP, Uike became a Rajya Sabha member in 2006. After that, she was a member of the National Commission for Women and Scheduled Tribes Commission. Presently she is the Governor of Chhattisgarh.

Icon of subaltern Hindutva

Harish S Wankhede of JNU has brought out another innovative thesis. He wants us to see Droupadi Murmu as an Icon of subaltern Hindutva. A new political agenda based on Dalit-Adivasi cultural symbols is being projected. He writes that behind such hyper construction of 'Subaltern Hindutva' lies a persuasive political claim that the Dalits and Adivasis are not only benefiting immensely under the Modi regime on the political front but that their social and class conditions are also improving.[80]

The way the argument is presented is the writer's own, but as a reader of his opinion, I can say that the BJP, from the very beginning, has been trying to project itself as a party of those who have been left behind. Since 2014, the thrust has been on the marginalised and weaker section of society. The schemes that were offered to them created a sense of repose in them that the government of the day was giving them something now and might give them something more in the near future. They had already seen many Dalit leaders, OBC leaders and the leaders who offered something only to a certain community. There were few leaders who projected themselves as the leaders of the minority community. There was none who could include 'everyone' irrespective of caste, community and creed. That is why the nomination of Droupadi Murmu came to them, not as a surprise but another step in the direction already taken by the party under the leadership of Narendra Modi. In fact, there is a group of so-called left-liberals who are habituated to seeing every attempt of the present government as an exercise to promote "Hindutva". It is the effort of the government to help, protect and bring the poor and marginalised of each community forward so that they themselves try to help themselves with the assistance so provided. When the government helps someone to come up, the person who is being helped should take it with pride and dignity.

Therefore, labels such as this serve academic purposes only. After all, who is a subaltern? The term subaltern designates and identifies the colonial populations who are socially, politically, and geographically excluded from the hierarchy of power of an imperial colony and from the metropolitan homeland of an empire. This is not British India. We are free and lead a free life. There is no 'subaltern', and even if there is one, that one can speak. Similarly, the discussion on Hindutva too leads an ordinary reader nowhere.

Droupadi Murmu is an icon and she is there to inspire all. An ordinary man who aspires to be extraordinary will read the story of her life to get inspired. After a while, she will be treated as our respected 15th President. She will be one among those who inspired several generations.

Let me conclude with the considered opinion of Ivy Imogene Hansdak, a Santhal poet and associate professor at New Delhi's Jamia Millia Islamia University, "The elevation of a leader from a marginalised community or group does not necessarily mean that the entire community or group will benefit. The only thing I can dare to hope for is that the chequered history of India's tribal people might enter the public discourse through her. Though she lacks agency while in office, she can still be a catalyst for change simply by occupying the office of president."[81]

Future Perfect

It will be the desire and wish of almost all Indians to see Mahamahim Rashtrapati making her presence felt. She will have to carve out her distinct image in people's minds. There are many soothsayers and Cassandra who are bent on saying alarming things about her. Doubts have been raised by the opponents over the 'weight' of her political credentials, 'stature' and ability to deliver etc. But PM Narendra Modi said that she would be a "great president". His views are based on seeing her past accomplishments. The president of The BJP, Shri J P Nadda, is also of the view that in a year when India is marking 'Azadi Ka Amrit Mahotsav', it has made every Indian proud that the highest office of this land will be occupied by a self-made woman who belongs to a tribal community. The women of India find it empowering that a woman will be our next President. Murmu will be the first President of our nation to be born after Independence, which also gives an important message.

In our democratic set up, everyone has the right to aspire and occupy the highest office of the land. Droupadi Murmu was not foisted but was duly elected by the members of the legislatures and Parliament. She defeated Sri Yashwant Sinha. Therefore, her rise to the revered position is completely legitimate and it is totally unnecessary to find any fault in her.

Every President before her left a legacy. Dr APJ was very popular among Youth. Pranab da was famous for his erudite constitutional wisdom. Mahamahim Murmu will have to carve out her distinct profile as he had previously done when she was a governor. She was called a 'troubleshooter' and pacifier then. I am sure she will be accessible as before and will be able to do something great for her community too. She has to build her profile as the country's first tribal President and carve out a niche for her.

Stamp of her own

The opposition and their candidate Shri Yashwant Sinha for the post, had this point in his mind when he opposed her candidature that the country should not have a "rubber-stamp president". The President should not be under pressure from the government. "They believe India's Rashtrapati should not function with a mind of her or his own and should merely serve as a rubber stamp to do the government's bidding. I am proud to belong to the other ideology that is determined to save the Constitution and the Republic."[82]

The fact of the matter is that the Congress leaders were rubber-stamps of the Nehru-Gandhi family. The fact is that Dr Kalam, Ram Nath Kovind and Droupadi Murmu are all NDA's choices and they created history in the annals of the Indian democratic system. In the words of senior journalist Vinod Sharma, "Most Presidents of the Republic were men of substance with a stamp of their own. It would do us well not to judge the office by intermittent aberrations. While presidents cannot lead governments by their nose, they certainly can nudge them toward the constitutional scheme on seeing them go astray.[83]

As a governor she had shown her mettle, not once but so many times. She will prove her critics wrong in due course of time.

In the considered opinion of Sankarshan Thakur, "Modi likes to rule by personal writ, detests dissent, and covets cult-building of the 'India is Indira, Indira is India' resonance. Modi's fawning votaries have often done better; one of them called him the avatar of God. And how must you behave when an avatar has put you in office? We shouldn't pre-judge Draupadi Murmu or judge her by who brings her into office. We must expect of our would-be president just what the citizenry of a vibrant, pluralist, democratic republic should."[84]

I find it difficult to conclude without giving you a kind of brief summary of the entire chapter taking the carefully chosen words of 'irreverent, provocative, and opinionated' Shobhaa De. Droupadi Murmu's credentials cannot be doubted or questioned. In one stroke, the BJP-NDA government has once again established its shrewd political acumen. The former Jharkhand governor comes with the right "signalling" material, being a tribal Santhal woman, who has bravely coped with enormous personal tragedies after losing her husband and two sons. She is a mother to a daughter and has the respect of the entire nation for her service to society. The BJP can flash both cards proudly and legitimately — her appointment will successfully court Adivasi and women voters and show the world how progressive India is, if one can only overlook the obvious conflicts.[85]

❒

Chapter Seven

Indian Presidential Election-2022

There is much to celebrate in the election of Droupadi Murmu as the 15th President of India in the Amrit Mahotsav Year of Independence. In Murmu, the country not only has a Santhal tribal woman as the head of the state but also a leader from one of the country's poorest regions. Her rise from the tribal lands of Western Odisha to become the first citizen is a glowing tribute to the success of Indian democracy.

—Ram Madhav

The last chapter of this book is under your scan now. This chapter is 'last but not the least.' This is the tale of a lifetime. Droupadi Murmu, a tribal lady, reaching the President's residence in Raisina Hills from her native village Rairangpur is a complicated one. In fact, the election of the President is not an ordinary one.

So far so good

On 10th July 2022, the outgoing President Shri Ram Nath Kovind presented his memoirs and wistfully wondered what more could have been accomplished. He was the 14th President of the country and now the country has got its 15th President. But elections were held 16 times. Would you not like to know about this process of election?

Lest we forget, let us recollect. Dr Rajendra Prasad became the first President of independent India. The Constitution of India was adopted on 26 January 1950 after about two and a half years of independence. The Constituent Assembly elected Dr Rajendra Prasad as the first President of India. Dr Prasad was the President of the Constituent Assembly. The first presidential election was held in 1952. Dr Rajendra Prasad got the victory in this, though the total number of candidates was five. He defeated K T Shah, who got a total of 92827 votes. Dr Prasad got 605386 votes. When the re-elections were held in 1957, Dr Rajendra Prasad was elected the President again. Hari Ram came second and got only 2672 votes.

The third presidential election was held in 1962. There were three candidates in total. In this election, the same Hari Ram lost again but remained at number two. He got 6341 votes this time. Dr Sarvepalli Radhakrishnan was elected the President of the country. The fourth presidential election was held in 1967. The total number of candidates was 17. This time the vote value of MPs increased as the 1961 census was taken care of. The total number of voters had also gone up to 4131. Dr Zakir Hussain defeated Koka Subbarao in this election. It is clear that he was the first Muslim President of India.

The fifth presidential election was held in 1969. This election was unprecedented in itself. The winner could not be declared by priority vote in the presidential election. All the candidates were eliminated except V V Giri and Neelam Sanjiva Reddy; later V V Giri was declared the winner. The sixth presidential election was held in 1974. This time the total number of candidates was 2 as the condition of 10 voters being proposers and 10 voters being seconders were added due to the presence of many non-serious candidates. The security deposit was also increased to Rs 2500, in this election Tridib Choudhary stood second and Fakhruddin Ali Ahmed was declared the President. The seventh presidential election was held in 1977. In this, the nominations of 36 candidates were rejected by the Returning Officer. There was no need for elections. Neelam Sanjeeva Reddy was declared the winner.

Other than Neelam Sanjeev Reddy, no other leader including Dr Rajendra Prasad, Dr Radhakrishnan, or Dr Zakir Hussain himself, took any initiative to become the President. Even the elected leaders after him never ever imagined that he/she would reach the highest office in the country.

The eighth presidential election was won in 1982 by the first Sikh, Giani Zail Singh by defeating HR Khanna. In the ninth Presidential Election which was held on July 16, 1987, R Venkataraman won by securing 7,40,148 votes over his nearest rival, VR Krishna Iyer, who got 2,81,550 votes.

The 10th Presidential Election was held on July 16, 1992. The winner Shankar Dayal Sharma secured 6,75,864 votes, while his nearest rival, George Gilbert Swell, got 3,46,485 votes. The 11th Presidential election, which was held on July 17, 1997, witnessed a record which is still unbroken. In that election, KR Narayanan got 9,56,290 votes, which is to date the highest ever in the Presidential Election of our country. His nearest rival, TN Seshan, got just 50,631 votes. Narayanan became the first Dalit to become the President of India. In this election, the ECI increased the security deposit from Rs 2,500 to

Rs 15,000, and the number of proposers and seconders increased from 10 to 50.

The 12th Presidential Election was held on July 15, 2002. Dr APJ Abdul Kalam, who won the election, came close to breaking the record of KR Narayanan by securing 9,22,884 votes. His rival Lakshmi Sahgal got 107,366 votes. The 13th Presidential Election was held on July 19, 2007. Pratibha Patil won the election by securing 6,38,116 votes, while her nearest rival, Bhairon Singh Shekhawat, got 3,31,306 votes. Pratibha Devi Singh Patil became the first female President of India. The 14th Presidential Election was held on July 19, 2012. The two leading candidates for the presidency were former Finance Minister Pranab Mukherjee from West Bengal and former Speaker of the Lok Sabha Purno Agitok Sangma from Meghalaya. The winner of the election, Pranab Mukherjee, got 7,13,763 votes while PA Sangma got 3,15,987 votes. The last Presidential Election, or the 15th one, was held on July 17, 2017. Ram Nath Kovind, former Bihar Governor and BJP leader, secured 7,02,644 votes and defeated Meira Kumar, who got 3,67,314 votes. Thus, Ram Nath Kovind became the second Dalit President of India.

The presidency of Ram Nath Kovind began on July 25, 2017, when he took the oath as the 14th President of India, administered by Chief Justice Jagadish Singh Khehar. Kovind was the Bharatiya Janata Party (BJP) (BJP)-led National Democratic Alliance (NDA) nominee and defeated the Indian National Congress (Congress)-led United Progressive Alliance (UPA) nominee and former speaker of Lok Sabha, Meira Kumar. The tenure of President Ram Nath Kovind came to an end on July 24, 2022.

Election-2022

As it was already decided that the tenure of President Ram Nath Kovind will come to an end on July 24, 2022, and as per Article 62 of the Constitution, an election to fill the vacancy caused by the expiration of the term of office was required to be completed before the term ends. Election Commission announced the schedule for Presidential Elections 2022. The ECI has fixed the schedule for the election of the office of the President of India. The notification for the election was issued on June 15; the last date for the nomination was scheduled for June 29, while the polls were to be held on July 18. The counting of votes was scheduled on 21st July, 2022.

In this context, the current Prime Minister Narendra Modi and his party suggested the name of Droupadi Murmu for the President's post. The opposition candidate Yashwant Sinha has been an extremely ambitious politician. Apart from holding a government administrative job, he has been associated with several political parties and held ministerial posts and power. From time to time, He was in the good books of several political leaders such as V.P. Singh, Chandrashekhar, Rajiv Gandhi, Narasimha Rao, Atal Bihari Vajpayee and L.K. Advani. With the help of the unity of the opposition and the strength of the regional parties, every effort was made to make Yashwant Sinha victorious. But Modi ji changed the whole game by making Droupadi Murmu a candidate. He spoiled their entire game. Yashwant Sinha's candidature became very frail in front of him. And Draupadi Murmu had a spectacular victory.

A presidential election was held in India on 18th July 2022 with the votes counted and the results announced on 21st July 2022. Let us look at it in detail now.

Opposition Decides and declares

Gopalkrishna Gandhi was approached first. It is amusing to read what he said before turning down the proposal, "Having considered the matter deeply, I see that the Opposition's candidate should be one who will generate a national consensus and a national atmosphere, besides Opposition unity. I feel there will be others who will do this far better than I."

Sharad Pawar, who is said to be always the bridesmaid, never the bride too, refused the offer. Farooq Abdullah also was not in a position to say, "I do agree," to be their offer. Finally, there was the fourth choice. He was Yashwant Sinha.

The opposition leaders held two rounds of discussions on Mr Sinha's name the night before and the morning before the main meeting which began at 2.30 PM on the 21st of June 2022. The leaders of Congress, Trinamool, Left, NCP, and Dravida Munnetra Kazhagam (DMK), met on the night before 21st June. There, Congress and the Left said that Mr Sinha would have to step down from the Trinamool party's post before announcing his name. Mamata Banerjee's party agreed on the same.

21st June 2022

On the morning of the 21st June, the final discussion on Mr Sinha's name was held at Pawar's house in consultation with M. Kharge of Congress, S. Yechuri of Communist Party of India Marxist (CPI M), D. Raja of CPI and Prafulla Patel of NCP. After the name was finalized, Mamta Banerjee spoke on the phone with Samajwadi Party (SP) leader Akhilesh Yadav, Rashtriya Janata Dal (RJD) leader Tejaswi Yadav, Aam Aadmi Party's (AAP) Aravind Kejriwal, Telangana Rashtra Samithi (TRS) leader, K.C. Rao (KCR), etc.

On the early hours of 21st June 2022, Mr Yashwant Sinha tweeted, "I am grateful to Mamtaji for giving me respect and dignity in the Trinamool Congress. Now is the time to move away from my political party in the greater national interest and to work for stronger opposition unity. I am sure she will approve of my move."

The opposition camp declared Yashwant Sinha as their Presidential candidate on the afternoon of the 21st of June 2022. After a series of meetings, the opposition's unanimous candidate in the Presidential election was Yashwant Sinha, a former Vajpayee-era Union Minister, and recent-former Trinamool Congress (TMC) Vice- President. The announcement on the part of the opposition was made in a joint statement after a one-and-a-half-hour meeting of 18 opposition parties convened by Nationalist Congress Party (NCP) leader Sharad Pawar.

NDA nominates

The NDA was also not sitting idle and there was also fast work going on since the morning of 21st June 2022. Shri Venkaiyya Naidu, the Vice President of India, who was on a three-day visit to Hyderabad, was summoned immediately to Delhi on the same day. He cut short his visit and came back to Delhi. Shri Amit Shah, Shri J.P. Nadda and others went to Shri Naidu's residence at noon.

The activity made the people guess that Mr Naidu might be considered a Presidential candidate by NDA. But, it is said that they went to his residence to inform him that he was not being considered for the President's post. Later in the evening, the leaders of the parliamentary board of BJP sat in a meeting in the presence of the Prime Minister. About 20 names were discussed there, leading to the green signal given to Droupadi Murmu's candidature. She was considered the most suitable candidate for the most prominent post.

Speaking at a press conference after the meeting, J.P Nadda said, "We wanted all parties to agree on a candidate. But the opposition has announced its candidate today. Therefore, we have also finalized the name of the NDA's candidate after discussing with the ally-party today."

Mr Nadda announced Droupadi Murmu's name as a Presidential candidate keeping in mind the representation of Eastern India, tribal society and women's society. In his words, "Droupadi Murmu, like Sarvapalli Radhakrishnan, has been teaching for a long time. After that, she came into politics. She was first a Counselor, then MLA and also the Minister of Transport, Trade and Fisheries in the Government of Orissa (jointly of BJP and BJD). She received the Nilkantha Award for best MLA in 2007." He noted that under the leadership of Prime Minister Narendra Modi, it was an honour to announce her as the Presidential candidate from NDA. "Her personality is an inspiration to us all and a benchmark for us all to follow.

It was thought that they agreed to offer her the candidature because the NDA had about 2 percent fewer votes than the Presidential vote required to win and they believed that the BJD would certainly vote for her as she hailed from their state. There was a social and political message in the election of the candidate of the NDA, which was completely absent in the case of the selected candidate of the opposition.

Her nomination and election signals the launch of Modi's preparations for the 2024 Lok Sabha elections. In terms of symbolism, Modi must have found that Murmu has political utility across several states. Scheduled Tribes constitute 14.8 per cent and 5.7 per cent of the population in Gujarat and Himachal Pradesh, respectively. These states will go to the polls this year. And out of nine states that go to polls next year, four are in the northeast where tribals play a decisive role — Nagaland (86.5 per cent), Meghalaya (86.1 per cent) and Tripura (31.8 per cent) in February and Mizoram (94.4 percent) in November. Tribals constitute seven per cent of the population in Karnataka that will go to polls in May next year. Of the four states that go to polls in November, tribals constitute 30.6 percent of the population in Chhattisgarh, 21.1 per cent in Madhya Pradesh, 13.5 per cent in Rajasthan and 9 per cent in Telangana. Tribals constitute around 23 per cent of the population in Odisha. It is Murmu's home state. Odisha will go to assembly polls along with the Lok Sabha election in 2024. Maharashtra is slated to go to polls in October 2024 and Jharkhand will go to polls in November 2024. Haryana will go to the polls along with Maharashtra. All these states have more than 9 percent tribal population. Even if symbolic, the utility factor of Mrs Murmu's elevation as the president of the Republic is immense.

The Media reacts

Droupadi Murmu's election as the fifteenth President of India was welcomed by the media throughout the country with great interest and enthusiasm. In fact, even before her name was announced, senior columnists and editors were suggesting her name as one of the choices. The party had considered 20 names before unanimously deciding on Murmu's name. Other than Droupadi Murmu; the party had considered senior leaders such as current Vice-President Venkaiah Naidu; governor of Chhattisgarh, Anusuiya Uikey; governor of Haryana, Bandaru Dattatreya; and governor of Telangana and lieutenant governor of Puducherry, Tamilisai Soundararajan as its presidential candidate. But she was nominated as she was found to be the most suitable. It has been a trend that the Modi Government gives ample opportunities to women candidates for gubernatorial posts. The Modi Government has appointed eight women governors and Lieutenant Governors since 2014. Women leaders like Mridula Sinha, Draupadi Murmu, Najma Heptulla, Anandiben Patel, Baby Rani Maurya, Anusuiya Uikey, Tamilisai Soundararajan, and Kiran Bedi have been given a responsibility to work in Narendra Modi's government. Five out of the eight women governor appointments by the Modi government were from Scheduled Castes, Scheduled Tribes, Other Backward Classes (OBCs), and Minority communities.

As I said, senior columnists and editors were suggesting her name as one of the choices. On May 10, 2022, nearly a month before the announcement of the Presidential Election Schedule for the 2022 election, "Prabhat Khabar" gave this news.

> Presidential election of India: Former Jharkhand Governor Droupadi Murmu can be made a BJP candidate. In the presidential election this time, the ruling BJP can give more importance to the Other Backward Classes (OBC) community and the women's section. The reason behind this is being told that a majority of people from the OBC community from Uttar Pradesh to Maharashtra and from Kashmir to Kanya Kumari. Former Jharkhand governor Droupadi Murmu is among the political figures being discussed as the candidates of the ruling BJP for this time's presidential election. The four names, including Droupadi Murmu, are being discussed by the BJP as the presidential candidate; the party's motive behind it is being told to cultivate the social and political equation of the 2024 Lok Sabha elections on the pretext of the presidential election.[86]

After that several newspapers gave their list of probable candidates and in almost all such forecasts her name was included. For instance, on June 14, a Bangalore based English newspaper wrote.

> Droupadi Murmu Another probable candidate for the BJP, Droupadi Murmu has proven her competency as an able administrator after being the only governor of Jharkhand to have completed a five-year term (2015-2021). A tribal leader from Odisha, she is the first woman governor of Jharkhand. She had been an Odisha cabinet minister and an MLA from the Rairangpur assembly constituency. Murmu came up as a possible candidate at the end of President Pranab Mukherjee's term as well. This time it is reported that the BJP might decide on Murmu's name to confirm its claims of working vigorously for the tribal population.[87]

Even the newspapers of the Middle-East were eager to forecast and foretell their inquisitive readers. "Gulfnews" published, "Murmu's candidature firmly buttresses the BJP narrative that it is a party that appeals to, and promotes leaders, other than those belonging to the upper castes. Murmu, a tribal leader, belonging to the Adivasi community — one of India's most marginal groups — is widely seen as a politically safe choice. This is a big boost to BJP's tribal push."[88]

Election Campaign-2022

Let me begin this section with an anecdote. In 1967, Zakir Husain was the presidential candidate from the ruling Congress party. The combined opposition had fielded Koka Subba Rao, a retired Chief justice of India. There was no campaign from either side. In fact, Dr Zakir Hussain was at the Michigan state university delivering the convocation address until three days before the election. When he was asked about the campaign, he smiled and quipped, "We in India only stand and do not run."

34 parties declared support for Opposition candidate Yashwant Sinha, while 44 for Droupadi Murmu. Droupadi Murmu's victory in this presidential election was certain, yet Yashwant Sinha, the candidate of the opposition party, insisted a lot. He also gave speeches. Both the candidates went across the country and campaigned for themselves. Mostly Sinha ji had to present his side in the campaign. Murmu continued to campaign with a calm spirit, but Yashwant Sinha became very agitated at times. Yashwant Sinha made many promises during the election campaign, like he said that he would fight against the CAA-NRC law till his last breath. If I win the

election, I will stop the misuse of investigating agencies. From the second day of taking the oath, this is what the agencies are doing on behalf of the government. Misuse is happening, and I will stop it. He also expressed his fear as to what would happen to him after the elections.

To garner support for the opposition party, the opposition leaders even went as far as to say that NDA's presidential candidate Droupadi Murmu represents the 'Evil Philosophy of India' or 'evil ideology' and should not be made a 'symbol of tribals.' Is this really a master stroke or is it just an initiative taken by the BJP for the upliftment of tribals? Murmu was called a "Murti', a statue. Murmu kept her dignity and decorum throughout the campaign.

Congress spokesperson Acharya Pramod Krishnam retweeted a statement by Yashwant Sinha, the joint presidential candidate on behalf of the opposition, and said – *Na No Man Tel Hoga, Na Radha Nachgi*. Yashwant Sinha will win the presidential election only then he will protect the constitution and will not allow the democratic values to be violated. There is no hope of his victory. Yashwant Sinha will win the presidential election only then he will protect the constitution and will not allow the democratic values to be violated. There is no hope of his victory. Naveen Patnaik not only strengthened the election of Droupadi Murmu as the next President of India, but also re-think many leaders who had little choice. Even Mamata Banerjee, an outspoken critic of Prime Minister Narendra Modi, was compelled. Shiv Sena chief Uddhav Thackeray was facing a similar dilemma and then he too agreed. The parties of Hemant Soren, Chirag Paswan Deve Gowda, Chandra Babu Naidu, Mayawati, Rajbhar, Jagan Mohan

Reddy etc all came together in favor of Murmu. National Democratic Alliance with the support of regional parties like Biju Janata Dal, Yuvajan Shramik Rythu-Congress Party, Bahujan Samaj Party, All India Anna Dravida Munnetra Kazhagam, Telugu Desam Party, Janata Dal-Secular, Shiromani Akali Dal, Shiv Sena and Jharkhand Mukti Morcha Candidate Draupadi Murmu's vote share jumped to nearly two-thirds in the presidential election to be held on July 18 and she became the first woman president of a tribal community. "The decision to vote was taken considering her background and the community she represents. It's not about this party or that party. Support is for the candidate." Saying this, many leaders supported Draupadi Murmu, not the BJP. But that was just her point of view. A senior leader rightly said, "When for the first time (presidency). If a tribal woman candidate is offered, why would anyone object? Any attempt to oppose the verdict will not send a good message to the tribals of our state."

Droupadi Murmu spoke politely. Somewhere someone was called brother and somewhere someone told the story of his life. Here are excerpts from the same speech he gave before MPs and MLAs in Jaipur. It has all that she kept saying while speaking in other places as well.

> Visiting the pink city of Jaipur is as pleasant as speaking your mind and heart among your loved ones. Despite the difference in geographical conditions in Rajasthan and Odisha, there are many similarities between the two states. In which to live with nature, people of Rajasthan keep water like life, similarly people of Odisha know how to keep the wheel of life spinning with new hope in spite of cyclonic storms.

There is a Rajasthani proverb that 'Ammar ko taro-haath se kauni tute', from where I have come, I understand the practicality of this proverb. The experience of my life journey so far says that nothing happens spontaneously, the struggles of the past remain connected with our today. Conflicts keep us conscious of purpose and resolutions.

Water, forest, land and tribals are now becoming the main participants of a secure and developing system. In the last several years, with the advancement in the lives of the downtrodden, the oppressed and the tribals, major changes have taken place. Development is now reaching remote areas equally. For the first time after independence, making a daughter of a tribal society as the candidate for the President, the living example of which is the respect of all the tribal brothers and sisters of the country.

Getting the office of President will not be my personal achievement; it will not be a matter of pride for any one place, community or society. This will prove to be an example of inclusive unity in Indian society arising out of the flow of Antyodaya. Geo-cultural plurality gives us individual identity, but basically, the more than 125 crore 'is' together become 'we' as Indians.

We are the children of Mother India holding the flag of unity in diversity. He said that coming to Marudhara, there is a wish to apply the soil of Haldighati on the forehead, where the brave Shiromani Maharana Pratap and tribal Jannayak Rana Poonja Bhil had fought against a bigger army than themselves under one flag to protect self-respect.

The heroes of Rajasthan put the protection of the motherland and the security of women's honour in the top priority of the government. He has got heroism not only in the state and in the country but also globally. This is the reason that the list of names of Ranbankurs is not the end in this state, which puts self-respect in the forefront of life values; the expansion is the expansion.

When I was made the presidential candidate on behalf of NDA and supporting parties, I could understand the thinking behind it, because I had an interview with the sensitive consciousness and visionary thinking of Honourable Prime Minister Narendra Modi. He wants to see the book and pen in the hands of the mother and daughter of the desert and is committed to bring the mother and daughter of the forest land into the mainstream. I am very happy that under the rule of the Modi government, water is reaching the house of Nari Shakti from the tap. Along with this, by connecting the daughters of tribal society with education, they are getting the right to the freedom to dream.

A daughter of a tribal society who grew up with small dreams in Odisha was given a way to reach Rashtrapati Bhavan, this is a democratic dream, and this is Antyodaya. This is to show faith in the daughter of the village, the poor and the jungle. Through the MPs and MLAs present here, I am seeking the support of the godlike people of Rajasthan. I never thought of becoming the President, but the NDA under the leadership of Prime Minister Narendra Modi has made me a medium to connect the people of the last villages in the mainstream. The deprived, the tribal and the exploited can see themselves in me. There is no difference, no difference between us. We are hopeful, forward and confident of building a New India.[89]

Presidential Election Polling-2022

The polling for the Presidential elections 2022 was held on July 18 between 10 am to 5 pm at the 31 locations. As per the Election Commission of India(ECI), over 99 per cent of the total 4796 electors cast their votes in Presidential polls, while 10 states and the union territory of Puducherry recorded a turnout of 100 per cent. Out of a total of 771 Members of Parliament entitled to vote (05 vacant) and similarly out of total 4025 Members of the Legislative Assemblies entitled to vote (06 vacant and 02 disqualified), over 99% cast their votes today. However, 100% voting by MLAs was reported from Chattisgarh, Goa, Gujarat, Himachal Pradesh,

Kerala, Karnataka, Madhya Pradesh, Manipur, Mizoram, Puducherry, Sikkim and Tamil Nadu.

Election Results

In the month of July

Everything was bright

After darkness light

Yashwant lost sight

Droupadi Murmu won the fight

The best and the last

From the word go, Droupadi Murmu was a shoo-in, and poor Yashwant Sinha was a goner from the word go. She found backers across party lines along her campaign trail. She had overwhelming numbers in her favour. There was no doubt about her victory. It was a cake-walk for her. Several glass-ceilings shattered in one go.

The NDA's presidential candidate Droupadi Murmu was officially declared as the 15th President of the country after the conclusion of the counting of votes on July 21, 2022. Murmu received 2,824 votes with a value 6,76,803 while her opponent Yashwant Sinha secured 1,877 votes with a value 3,80,177. A total of 4,809 MPs and MLAs cast their votes in the polling that took place on July 18. Presidential Election concluded with the declaration of the result...4754 votes polled, out of which 4701 were valid & 53 invalid. The quota (for a candidate to be elected the President) was 5,28,491. Droupadi Murmu secured 2824 first preference votes-value of which is 6,76,803. 1,877 first preference votes were secured by Yashwant Sinha – value 3,80,177. Amid heavy cross-voting she received 64.03% of total valid votes polled. The massive cross-voting is an indication of the depletion in the opposition camp. They were scattered and confused. Around 125 MLAs and 17 MPs from different assemblies and constituencies cross-voted in her support.

As 1st preference votes secured by Droupadi Murmu were greater than the requisite quota, Droupadi Murmu was declared elected to the office of President of India.

"India scripts history. At a time when 1.3 billion Indians are marking Azadi Ka Amrit Mahotsav, a daughter of India hailing from a tribal community born in a remote part of eastern India has been elected our President!" the PM said in a tweet. You and I too join the PM in congratulating her for her victory. We wish and hope that as the 15th President of India, she functions as the Custodian of the Constitution without fear or favour.

The Oath Taking Ceremony

When Droupadi Murmu takes oath on 25th July 2022, her age is 64 years and 35 days. The record of being the youngest President so far is in the name of Neelam Sanjiva Reddy. His age was 64 years, two months and 6 days. She is the representative of New India, a young India. Debabrata Mohanty from Uperbeda/Rairangpur has got some anecdotal material to share with you. He meets a 63-year-old lady who used to be Droupadi Murmu's classmate in 1964. Her name is Tapti Mandal. She didn't know it then but knows well now that the President of India is her childhood friend. Let us also read the story published in The Hindustan Times.

> The teacher asked students to recite a poem, and the topper volunteered again. Mandal knew which poem was coming, and why. The verses were from an Odia translation of Robert Frost's *Stopping by Woods on a Snowy Evening*. In the run up to that day, the teacher had told his wards that the poem was Jawaharlal Nehru's favourite, famously kept on his bedside table. Young Tudu was taken by the reference. So when her friend finished the last stanza with the words, "there are miles to go before I sleep", Mandal recalls mocking her, she asked her classmate if she planned to become a leader like India's first Prime Minister.
>
> "I laugh when I think about that day. Perhaps, even then, she was predicting her own future," Mandal says.

A nine-year-old Tudu turned to Mandal, her eyes fiery. "Why not?" She asked.

Why not, indeed. Fifty-five years later, on July 21, 64-year-old Droupadi Tudu, now Droupadi Murmu, became the 15th President of India, and the country's first woman tribal commander-in-chief.[90]

Such are the tales that make narratives and create poignant pictures. When the youth of the present generation, like Aditi Narayani Paswan, reads it, they say, "This poignant picture has inspired many young women from marginalized communities, like me, to dream big. Droupadi Murmu is not just a source of inspiration for us; her life and struggle, determination, and success in the face of great odds represent the hope and promise of New India."[91]

Her journey from a humble beginning in Rairangpur to becoming a resident of Raisina Hills is indeed inspiring. It is a glittering example of women's empowerment. India got its first tribal President. We hope and pray to God that the new President will guide our country forward and protect our values enshrined in our constitution. We, the people, are thankful to one and all.

The woods are lovely, dark and deep,
But I have promises to keep,
And miles to go before I sleep,

Afterword

I didn't write the preface of this book. I couldn't. I was so overwhelmed with the spontaneous overflow of powerful feelings that it was beyond me to thank anyone or acknowledge the contribution of any soul other than my own self. It was a tremendous experience. I wanted to dedicate this book to my younger son Anshul Sharma as on 25th of July it was his birthday and I was devoting all my time in writing these lines. I wished to dedicate this book to my grandson Arayav and Droupadi Murmu's granddaughters as they will be the readers of this book one day. The thought of writing an afterword occurred to me on the morning of 26th July when the publisher of the book Shri Narender Kumar Verma reminded me to send the book's preface.

I would like to mention something for my satisfaction with a recommendation to you to read the bulky autobiography of Dr. Rajendra Prasad, the first President of the country, on the Amrit Mahotsav of our Independence. Rajendra Babu got his autobiography published two to four months before the country's independence. The foreword was written by Iron Man Sardar Patel. He wrote in the foreword, "On seeing Shri Rajendra Babu, the impression of his simplicity and humility that falls on our hearts, his reflection is found in the pages of this autobiography."

("shree raajendr baaboo ko dekhate hee unakee saralata aur namrata kee jo chhaap hamaare dil par padatee hai, usaka pratibimb is aatmakatha ke panne panne mein paaya jaata hai.") And the grateful and dutiful Babu Rajdendra Prasad too wrote on 8 January 1947 in the one page-preface of his detailed biography, "The readers will like it or not, they only know. (paathak ise pasand karenge ya nahin, ye vahee jaanen.)

I too would like to say the same for my book just concluded. Thank you!

In a watershed moment, Droupadi Murmu was sworn in as the 15th President of India. She became the second woman President of the country and the first-ever tribal woman to hold the highest Constitutional post in India. As soon as Droupadi Murmu was sworn in as the country's first tribal President at exactly 10:15 on 25th July 2022, the central hall of the Parliament building reverberated with applause. Droupadi Murmu, the country's new President, gave a speech in Hindi in her natural style. In her address, there was a glimpse of tribal society. Her address was rich in the invocation of India's tribal legacy. She started her maiden speech with the traditional tribal greeting of 'Johar' and ended it by quoting famous Odia saint and poet Bhim Bhoi. She also underlined the tribal community's magnificent role in the country's freedom struggle by mentioning Santhal, Paika, Kol, and Bhil revolutions. The former Prime Minister Atal Bihari Vajpayee was also mentioned. She said that her election to the highest constitutional post of the country was proof that the poor of India could dream and fulfill it. She said that she started her life journey from a small tribal village in Odisha. From the background she comes from, it was also a dream for her to pursue elementary education, but despite many obstacles, she was determined and she was the first person in her village to go to college. The Central Hall of Parliament resonated with applause several times during the President's address.

The ever-active Wikipedia has added her in a befitting manner as they can.

> Droupadi Murmu (née Tudu, born 20th June 1958) is an Indian politician serving as the 15th and current President of India since 25th July 2022. She is a member of the Bharatiya Janata Party (BJP). She is the first person belonging to the indigenous, scheduled tribe community to be elected as the President of India.

Names do not die in Santhali culture

'The Telegraph' online tried to clarify her name. There has been so much talk about her maiden name. The magazine now claims that her name Droupadi, based on a character of the epic Mahabharata' was given by her school teacher. This is what they say in support of their claim. In an interview with an Odia video magazine some time ago, she revealed that her Santhali name Puti was changed to Droupadi by a teacher in school.

> Droupadi was not my original name. It was given by my teacher, who hailed from another district, not from my native Mayurbhanj. The teacher did not like my previous name and changed it for good. So my name was changed several times - from Durpadi to Dorpdi. Names do not die in Santhali culture. If a girl is born, she takes the name of her grandmother, while a son carries his grandfather's nomenclature.

These are the reports being found in the media, and one can appreciate when the result of all this is in the form of responses and admiration and congratulatory messages from one and all. Chinese President Xi Jinping congratulated Droupadi Murmu on assuming office, saying he stood ready to work with her to push ties forward. The Presidents of Russia, Sri Lanka, Bangladesh, the Maldives, and Nepal were among the other world leaders who greeted President Murmu. If I have to select only a few of the comments, I must include the words written by business tycoon Anand Mahindra. She hailed the President's exemplary courage and commitment to serve and cited her as his source of Monday motivation.

> "Look no further for your #MondayMotivation Above all else, she is a person of extraordinary courage and a commitment to serve. Her inner strength has enabled her to withstand all the challenges life has thrown at her. I join in saluting her. A moment of intense pride for India."

Johar, Nameskar

President Murmu started her speech with Johar, a word that is a salutation spoken by tribal people in the tribal regions of Chhattisgarh, Jharkhand and Odisha. Johar stands for "victory to all living and nonliving components of nature." "Johar" means "victory to the wellbeing of all." In this context, "Johar" means "Jai for the welfare of all," i.e., Johar is the spirit of absolute commitment to nature. Just like Namaskar, "Johar" is also used along with folded hands to greet people, or in case of elders, by touching their feet. Juhar" is also one of the rituals of Nuakhai, an agricultural festival celebrated to welcome the new crop. It is a combination of two words - 'nua' means 'new' and 'khai' means 'to eat'. The festival is celebrated primarily in Western Odisha, southern Chhattisgarh and adjoining areas of Simdega (in Jharkhand). Greeting the people of the country with "Johar, Namaskar", the President said in her tweet Indians' wishes would give her strength to fulfill her duties in the highest office.

No personal achievement

The President said that she belonged to the tribal society and she got the opportunity to become the President of India from Ward Counselor. This is the greatness of India, the mother of democracy. It is the power of democracy that in it, a tribal daughter of a poor household can reach the highest constitutional post of India. She said that reaching the post of President is not her personal achievement. This is the achievement of every poor person of India. Her election proves that the poor of India can dream and fulfill it.

She said that she was the first President of the country who was born in independent India. We will have to work at a fast pace in this noble period to fulfill the expectations that our freedom fighters had made from us citizens of independent India. In these 25 years, the path to accomplishment will proceed on two tracks – everyone's effort and duty.

Vote as an expression of faith

Earlier in the beginning of her address, the President thanked all the MPs and members of the Legislative Assembly for being elected to the highest constitutional post of India. She said that their vote is an expression of the faith of crores of citizens of the country. She humbly greeted all the countrymen from the holy Parliament for the hopes, aspirations, and rights of all the citizens of India. 'Your affinity, trust, and your support will be my great strength in fulfilling this new responsibility for me.' She said.

Amrit Mahotsav

She said that the country has elected her as the President at such an important period when we are celebrating the Amrit Mahotsav of our independence. A few days from today, the country will complete 75 years of its independence. It is also a coincidence that when the country was celebrating the 50th anniversary of its independence, then her political career started, and today, in the 75th year of independence, she has got this new responsibility. It is a great privilege for her to be given this responsibility.

Environment and Nature

She said that she was born in that tribal tradition which has carried life in harmony with nature for thousands of years. She has realized the importance of forests and water bodies in her life. We take necessary resources from nature and serve nature with equal reverence.

Citing the Poet

Towards the end of her address when Murmu said she has "realised the meaning of life only through public service", she quoted a poet.In her life so far, she said, she has experienced the meaning of life in public service. There is a line from the poem of Bhim Bhoi ji, an eminent poet of Jagannath Kshetra: *'Mo jeevan pache narke padi thau, jagat deliverance heu'*. According to the English translation published by the President's Secretariat, it means "working for the welfare of the world is far greater than one's own interests".

Bhima Bhoi was a Kondh tribal poet of Odisha. Sitakant Mahapatra, in his book on him, writes that Bhim Bhoi took Mahima Dharma to millions of people, which was founded by Mahima Swami. Though it was founded by Swami, he left behind no written works, and it was Bhim Bhoi who took Mahima traditions to the masses. The book noted, "It is possible to assert that, but for Bhima, Mahima Dharma would have at most remained a mere obscure philosophical cult with esoteric ideas about the void, the shapeless universal, the timeless entity, and so on. Bhim Bhoi's contribution in the making of Odia literature is unparalleled."

Dharti Aaba Bhagwan Birsa Munda

President Droupadi Murmu paid tribute to the freedom fighters of the country and their contribution to the freedom struggle of India. She hailed the patriotism of Bhagwan Birsa Munda and marked the relevance of the Tribal community in the freedom struggle of India. She stated that an outline of India's new journey has been prepared as a nation. Our freedom struggle is a continuous stream of those struggles and sacrifices which have played a major role in the Independence of India.

Standing for the Deprived

Murmu said that it is a matter of satisfaction for her that those who were deprived for centuries, kept away from the benefits of development, those poor, downtrodden, backward, and tribals can see their reflection in her. This election of hers includes the blessings of the poor of the country. It is a glimpse of the dreams and potential of crores of poor women and daughters of the country.

Invoking past Presidents

She said that from the first President of the country, Dr. Rajendra Prasad, to Shri Ram Nath Kovind ji, many eminent personalities have adorned this post. Along with this post, the country has also entrusted her with the responsibility of representing this great tradition. In the light of the Constitution, She will discharge her duties with utmost sincerity. For her, the democratic-cultural ideals of India and all the countrymen will always be her source of energy.

Mentioning Atal Bihari Vajpayee

The President said that she has closely observed the enthusiasm and self-confidence of the youth of the country. All of us revered Atal ji, who used to say that when the youth of the country move forward, they not only make their own destiny but also make the fate of the country. Today we are seeing it come true. He wanted all our sisters and daughters to be empowered more and more and they continue to increase their contribution in every field of the country.

Adding Sri Aurobindo

She said that decades ago she had the opportunity to work as a teacher in Sri Aurobindo Integral School in Rairangpur. A few days later, the 150th birth anniversary of Sri Aurobindo will be celebrated. Sri Aurobindo's ideas about education continue to inspire her.

Sri Aurobindo (born Aurobindo Ghose; 15 August 1872 – 5 December 1950) was an Indian philosopher, yoga guru, maharishi, poet, and Indian nationalist. He was also a journalist, editing newspapers such as Vande Mataram. He joined the Indian movement for independence from British colonial rule until 1910, was one of its influential leaders, and then became a spiritual reformer, introducing his visions on human progress and spiritual evolution. Aurobindo Ghosh comes out against the educational system of his time. He believes that education should be according to the mental and spiritual needs of the children and the demands of the country. It means that education should be in accordance with the changing and growing needs of our reality as well as modern life. He considers the fulfillment of swadharma as the law of life and wants that every individual in a nation should fulfill his swadharma. Hence, the purpose of education is to prepare the individual to serve their nation and humanity. He wrote, "Education to be true, must not be a machine made fabric; but true building or living evocation of the power of the mind and spirit of a human being." In the words of Mother, who was the closest collaborator of Sri Aurobindo, "To be complete education there must be five principle aspects relating to five principle activities of human beings: the physical, the mental, the psyche, the vital and the spiritual. This education is complete, complementary to each other and continues till the end of life." Sri Aurobindo used the sense of integral education in two dimensions. In the first dimension, integral means imparting five aspects (physical, mental, spiritual, vital, and psyche) of individual beings, and in the second sense of integral means, education is not for the evolution of individuals but for the nation and finally for humanity. In a broader sense, integral means the evolution of humanity and promoting the principle of unity in diversity.

Record-Breaker and Record-Maker

Droupadi Murmu took oath as the 15th President of the country. With this, the country got the first tribal and second woman president. With the swearing-in, not one or two but eight big records were broken or made by her.

1. **First Tribal President:** Murmu is the first tribal of the country to reach the post of President. Till date, no president has been nominated and elected from any tribal society. Not only this, Droupadi is a woman. Therefore, the record of being the first woman tribal president was also recorded in her name.
2. **The first president born after independence:** All the past presidents, including the 14th Shri Ram Nath Kovind, were born before independence, i.e., before 1947. Droupadi Murmu is the first President born after independence. She was born on 20th June 1958.
3. **Youngest President:** Droupadi Murmu, 64, is the youngest President of the country. Before her, this record was in the name of Neelam Sanjeeva Reddy. When Reddy became the President, he was 64 years and two months old. At the same time, on 25th July 2022. During the oath-taking ceremony, Droupadi Murmu's age is 64 years and a month.
4. **Second woman President:** Droupadi Murmu's name was also recorded for being the second woman President. Prior to her, Pratibha Devi Singh Patil was the President from 2007 to 2012. She was the first woman President of the country.

5. **First President from Odisha:** Till date no President was from Odisha. Droupadi Murmu will be the first President who hails from Odisha. Earlier, VV Giri was the President who was related to Odisha. Giri was born in Baharampur in Madras Presidency, now in Odisha. However, Giri belonged to a Telugu family. His constituency was in Andhra Pradesh. From there, he continued to become an MP.

6. **Second President to come from BJP background:** She will be the second President who comes from a Bharatiya Janata Party background. The previous President, Ram Nath Kovind, was the first President to come from a BJP background, whose entire political life was associated with the BJP.

7. **First Councilor to become President:** Droupadi Murmu is the first leader to become President, who has been a Councillor. She was a clerk. She was then a teacher. After that, she got into politics and was elected councilor in 1997. After three years, she reached the assembly. She has been a minister twice in the BJP-BJD government of Odisha. She is also the first tribal woman in the country to become the governor of a state.

8. **Fastest of them all-** Droupadi Murmu started her political career in 1997. She became the President of India in 2022. No other President before her reached there as fast as she could. She herself admitted in her speech that, "it is also a coincidence that my political career started when the country was celebrating its 50th year of independence." Just 25 years! Long live our republic!

References

1 https://economictimes.indiatimes.com/news/politics-and-nation/view-why-it-would-be-incorrect-to-limit-draupadi-murmus-nomination-to-notions-of-empowerment-and-emancipation/articleshow/92507578.cms?utm_source=contentofinterest&utm_medium=text&utm_campaign=cppst

2 https://openthemagazine.com/cover-stories/draupadi-murmu-an-epic-choice/

3 https://gulfnews.com/opinion/op-eds/draupadi-murmu-as-president-of-india-much-more-than-identity-politics-1.88883051

4 https://theprint.in/50-word-edit/draupadi-murmu-for-president-a-salute-to-indias-prideful-and-underserved-tribal-communities/1007495/

5 Ram Nath Kovind (2018) Gopal Sharma, Anugya, Page 175

6 Droupadi Murmu | The irresistible rise - The Hindu

7 https://www.youtube.com/watch?v=eeGLkOLH8cA

8 https://www.theweek.in/theweek/cover/2022/06/24/bjp-ticks-all-the-right-boxes-by-nominating-droupadi-murmu.html

9 https://www.oneindia.com/politicians/droupadi-murmu-39156.html

10 https://www.indiatoday.in/india/story/droupadi-murmu-native-village-in-odisha-rairangpur-1967835-2022-06-28

11 https://www.firstpost.com/opinion/presidential-poll-why-voting-against-draupadi-murmu-wont-be-easy-10886391.html

12 https://www.onmanorama.com/news/india/2022/06/24/droupadi-murmu-president-candidate-teacher-odisha.html

13 https://www.livehindustan.com/national/story-droupadi-murmu-hometown-ready-for-celebration-presidential-election-in-india-htgp-6821035.html?utm_source=EditNewsPerpetual

14 https://www.bbc.com/news/world-asia-india-61892776

15 https://theprint.in/opinion/not-a-rubber-stamp-in-droupadi-murmus-backyard-the-hunger-for-development-has-a-got-a-boost/1043665/

16 https://www.indiatoday.in/india/story/everyone-will-support-if-they-come-to-know-her-droupadi-murmu-s-daughter-1965954-2022-06-23

17 https://www.indiatoday.in/india/story/everyone-will-support-if-they-come-to-know-her-droupadi-murmu-s-daughter-1965954-2022-06-23

18 https://www.thehitavada.com/Encyc/2022/6/24/Draupadi-Murmu-a-tenacious-teacher.html

19 https://www.news18.com/news/politics/draupadi-murmu-maam-ate-at-roadside-stalls-travelled-sans-security-assam-bjp-worker-recounts-2006-meet-5496421.html

20 https://www.jagran.com/jharkhand/jamshedpur-draupadi-murmu-news-the-journey-from-rairangpur-to-raisina-hills-rashtrapati-bhavan-was-not-easy-for-draupadi-murmu-22826268.html

21 Droupadi Murmu overcomes triple tragedy to emerge as President candidate | Bhubaneswar News - Times of India (indiatimes.com)

22 https://www.bbc.com/news/world-asia-india-61892776

23 https://www.theweek.in/theweek/cover/2022/06/24/bjp-ticks-all-the-right-boxes-by-nominating-droupadi-murmu.html

24 https://www.newindianexpress.com/nation/2022/jun/23/murmus-spiritual-calling-at-mount-abu-2468663.html

https://www.youtube.com/watch?v=vlxLbGWh4b4

25 https://www.aajtak.in/lifestyle/women/story/draupadi-murmu-sworn-in-as-first-woman-governor-of-jharkhand-298593-2015-05-18

26 https://indianexpress.com/article/india/jharkhand-recalls-droupadi-murmus-stint-down-to-earth-and-an-accessible-governor-7983168/

27 https://theprint.in/politics/droupadi-murmu-nda-presidential-pick-is-ex-professor-took-bjp-head-on-as-jharkhand-governor/1007966/

28 Droupadi Murmu: A gentle conciliator - The Hindu BusinessLine

29 https://www.shethepeople.tv/news/droupadi-murmu-president-candidate/

30 https://www.bbc.com/news/world-asia-india-61892776

31 https://indianexpress.com/article/india/the-sunday-profile-droupadi-murmu-raisina-calling-8033868/

32 https://timesofindia.indiatimes.com/city/bhubaneswar/moms-hard-work-integrity-have-taken-her-to-where-she-is-today-says-droupadi-murmus-daughter/articleshow/

33 https://indianexpress.com/article/india/the-sunday-profile-droupadi-murmu-raisina-calling-8033868/

34 https://timesofindia.indiatimes.com/city/bhubaneswar/moms-hard-work-integrity-have-taken-her-to-where-she-is-today-says-droupadi-murmus-daughter/articleshow/

35 https://theprint.in/opinion/not-a-rubber-stamp-in-droupadi-murmus-backyard-the-hunger-for-development-has-a-got-a-boost/1043665/

36 https://hindi.oneindia.com/fact-check/fact-check-president-candidate-droupadi-murmu-does-not-have-any-twitter-account

37 https://tfipost.com/2022/06/this-is-why-we-need-droupadi-murmu-as-the-president-of-india/

38 https://www.indiatoday.in/india-today-insight/story/how-droupadi-murmu-walked-the-long-path-from-rairangpur-to-the-brink-of-being-elected-to-the-nation-s-highest- -public-office-1966498-2022-06-24&oq=ow-

39 https://rajbhavanjharkhand.nic.in/Speech/sp-050715a.pdf

40 https://www.indiaherald.com/Editorial/Read/994511763/Droupadi-Murmu-BJP-has-got-second-Kalam

41 https://indianexpress.com/article/india/tribal-at-top-people-will-have-faith-in-system-in-murmus-town-pride-and-hope-7985487/

42 https://www.telegraphindia.com/india/odisha-droupadi-murmus-fight-against-the-odds/cid/1871681

43 https://odishabytes.com/my-mother-will-be-an-inspiration-for-santhals-says-droupadi-murmus-daughter

44 https://www.indiatoday.in/india/story/-shared-cordial-relations-with-didi-ex-jmm-droupadi-murmu-1966399-2022-06-24

45 https://www.indiatvnews.com/astrology/draupadi-murmu-kundali-raja-yog-bjp-presidential-candidate-horoscope-will-she-win-prediction-2022-07-01-788896

46 https://twitter.com/narendramodi/status/1539282555198771201

47-48 Collected Works of M.K. Gandhi, vol. 95: 347-348.

49-50 *"CADIndia". Cadindia.clpr.org.in. Archived from the original on 23 June 2022.*

51 https://swarajyamag.com/ideas/the-civilisational-importance-of-draupadi-murmu-becoming-indias-next-president

52 For BJP, the Optics of Nominating the First Tribal Woman President Couldn't Be Better (thewire.in)

53 https://www.opindia.com/2022/06/indian-left-casts-aspersions-on-credentials-of-tribal-leader-draupadi-murmu/

54 Could Venkaiah Naidu Have Served the BJP Well as Presidential Candidate? (thewire.in)

55 https://organiser.org/2022/06/23/87576/bharat/vanvasi-kalyan-ashram-endorses-draupadi-murmu-as-bharats-next-president-congratulates-pm-nda-for-historic-decision/

56 https://www.news9live.com/opinion-blogs/draupadi-murmu-president-for-the-right-reasons-178598?infinitescroll=1

57 https://www.newslaundry.com/2022/06/23/tribal-ties-east-india-outreach-sulking-allies-why-droupadi-murmu-ticks-all-boxes-for-bjp

58 https://www.thehindu.com/news/national/explained-the-context-and-import-of-mahasweta-devis-draupadi/article36131705.ece

59 https://gulfnews.com/opinion/op-eds/draupadi-murmu-as-president-of-india-much-more-than-identity-politics-1.88883051

60 https://www.sundayguardianlive.com/opinion/pm-modi-naming-murmu-presidents-post-masterstroke

61 https://www.deccanchronicle.com/opinion/dc-comment/230622/dc-edit-murmu-as-prez-will-be-a-matter-of-pride-for-india.html

62 https://indianexpress.com/article/opinion/columns/aditi-narayani-paswan-writes-droupadi-murmu-candidature-politics-representation-tokenism-7999113/

63 Opposition leader told me 'PM twice, what more', but I can't rest: Narendra Modi | India News,The Indian Express

64 https://ianslive.in/news/prez_poll_draupadi_murmu_s_nomination_tactical_outreach_to_tribals-882590/NATION/1

65 The Droupadi Murmu Masterstroke: How BJP Manages Three Gains with One Action | OPINION (thequint.com)

66 http://timesofindia.indiatimes.com/articleshow/89416310.cms?utm_source=contentofinterest&utm_medium=text&utm_campaign=cppst

67 https://timesofindia.indiatimes.com/india/bjp-slams-yashwant-sinha-says-his-appeal-to-murmu-depicts-nasty-mindset/articleshow/92652145.cms

68 https://www.telegraphindia.com/india/bjp-slams-yashwant-sinha-says-his-appeal-to-murmu-depicts-nasty-mindset/cid/1873098

69 Gopal Sharma, Kamala D Harris, Dimond Books.

70 https://indianexpress.com/article/opinion/aditi-narayani-paswan-writes-droupadi-murmu-candidature-politics-representation-tokenism-7999113/

71 Dhuni Soren, History of Santals (2019) page 20-21

72 Ram Nath Kovind: The Republican Ethic (2018) Selected Speeches (July 2017-July 2018), Publications Divisions.

73-74 https://www.news18.com/news/politics/presidential-polls-ktr-compares-draupadi-to-bhishma-backs-yashwant-sinha-slams-dictatorial-bjp-5449087.html

75 https://scroll.in/article/1026797/droupadi-murmu-as-president-would-be-a-triumph-for-the-sangh-parivar-but-not-the-adivasi-community?utm_source=rss&utm_medium=public

76 https://www.outlookindia.com/national/draupadi-murmu-for-president-bjp-s-masterstroke-but-adivasi-women-need-more-than-symbolism--news-204021

77 https://lagatar24.com/droupadi-murmus-nomination-for-presidents-job-not-ornamental-has-civilisational-importance-tribal-affairs-minister-arjun-munda/104074/

78 https://www.deccanchronicle.com/opinion/dc-comment/230622/dc-edit-murmu-as-prez-will-be-a-matter-of-pride-for-india.html

79 https://thesquadron.in/can-murmus-election-emancipate-the-tribals/

80 https://www.deccanherald.com/opinion/comment/droupadi-murmu-new-icon-of-subaltern-hindutva-1125499.html

81 https://www.dw.com/en/who-is-draupadi-murmu-indias-likely-next-president/a-62513878

82 https://thewire.in/politics/country-should-not-have-rubber-stamp-president-fight-is-ideological-yashwant-sinha

83 https://www.hindustantimes.com/opinion/distantly-close-a-look-back-at-droupadi-murmu-s-illustrious-predecessors-101656314534662.html

84 https://www.telegraphindia.com/opinion/hollow-voice-silence-has-been-a-virtue-for-indian-presidents/cid/1873381

85 https://www.asianage.com/opinion/columnists/250622/shobhaa-de-is-murmu-choice-as-prez-an-inspired-masterstroke-or.html

86 https://www.prabhatkhabar.com/national/former-jharkhand-governor-draupadi-murmu-may-be-bjp-candidate-in-presidential-election-in-india-vwt

87 https://www.deccanherald.com/national/presidential-election-2022-who-might-be-a-potential-candidate-1118111.html

88 https://gulfnews.com/opinion/op-eds/who-is-droupadi-murmu--bjps-candidate-for-the-president-of-india-1.88751440

89 https://www.patrika.com/jaipur-news/draupadi-murmu-said-salute-to-the-soil-of-haldighati-gave-speech-in-hindi-7651273/

90 https://www.hindustantimes.com/india-news/why-not-how-a-tribal-girl-who-dared-to-dream-became-india-s-15th-president-101658423534538.html

91 https://indianexpress.com/article/opinion/columns/aditi-narayani-paswan-writes-droupadi-murmu-candidature-politics-representation-tokenism-7999113/

President's Speech

Johar!

Namaskar!

I express my heartfelt gratitude to all Members of Parliament and Legislative Assemblies for electing me to the highest Constitutional post of India. Your vote for me is an expression of the faith of crores of citizens of the country. I humbly greet all the fellow citizens from this sacred Parliament, a symbol of the hopes, aspirations, and rights of all the citizens of India. Your affection, trust, and support will be my greatest strength in discharging my functions and responsibilities.

The country has elected me as the President at a crucial time when we are celebrating 'Azadi Ka Amrit Mahotsav'. A few days from today, the country will complete 75 years of its independence. It is also a coincidence that my political career started when the country was celebrating its 50th year of independence.

And today, in the 75th year of independence, I have been assigned this new responsibility. It is my great privilege to be given this responsibility at such a historic time when

India is engaged with full vigour in realising its vision for the next 25 years. I also happen to be the first President of the country who was born in independent India. We have to work at a fast pace in this Amritkal to fulfil the expectations of our freedom fighters from the citizens of independent India.

In these 25 years, the path to attain the goals of Amritkal will proceed on two tracks ***–Sabka Prayas aur Sabka Kartavya*** (everyone's effort and everyone's duty).

The new development journey towards the bright future of India has to be undertaken by our collective efforts, following the path of duty. We will be observing Kargil Vijay Diwas tomorrow i.e., July 26th. This day is a symbol of both- the bravery and restraint of the Indian armed forces. Today, I extend my best wishes in advance to the armed forces of the country and to all the citizens.

Ladies and Gentlemen,

I started my journey of life from a small tribal village in Odisha in the eastern part of the country. From the background that I come from, it was like a dream for me to get elementary education. But despite many obstacles, my determination remained strong and I became the first daughter of my village to go to college.

I belong to a tribal society. I have got the opportunity to rise from serving as a ward councillor to becoming the President of India. This is the greatness of India, the mother of democracy. It is a tribute to the power of our democracy that a daughter born in a poor house in a remote tribal area can reach the highest constitutional position in India.

That I attained the post of President is not my personal achievement, it is the achievement of every poor person in India. My election is proof of the fact that the poor in India can have dreams and fulfil them too.

And it is a matter of great satisfaction for me that those who have been deprived for centuries and those who have been denied the benefits of development, those poor, downtrodden, backwards, and tribals, are seeing their reflection in me.

This election of mine has the blessings of the poor of the country. And it reflects the dreams and potential of crores of women and daughters of the country.

This election of mine also shows the courage of today's youth of India, who is ready to walk on new paths and shun the beaten tracks.

Today I feel proud to lead such a progressive India. Today, I assure all fellow citizens, especially the youth of India and the women of India, that their interests will be paramount for me while working in this position.

Ladies and Gentlemen,

Before me is such a great legacy of the Presidency of India, which has continuously strengthened the prestige of Indian democracy in the world. From the country's first President, Dr. Rajendra Prasad, to Shri Ram Nath Kovind ji, stalwarts have adorned this post. Along with this post, the country has also entrusted me with the responsibility of representing this great tradition.

In the light of the Constitution, I will discharge my duties with utmost sincerity.

For me, the democratic-cultural ideals of India and all the citizens will always be my source of energy.

Ladies and Gentlemen,

Our freedom struggle had prepared the roadmap for India's new journey as a nation. Our freedom struggle was a continuous stream of those struggles and sacrifices which had nurtured so many ideals and possibilities for an independent India. Pujya Bapu had resorted to Swaraj, Swadeshi, Swachhta, and Satyagraha to show us the way for realising Indian cultural ideals.

Countless personalities like Netaji Subhash Chandra Bose, Nehru ji, Sardar Patel, Babasaheb Ambedkar, Bhagat Singh, Sukhdev, Rajguru and Chandrashekhar Azad had taught us to keep national pride as paramount. Many brave women icons like Rani Lakshmi Bai, Rani Velu Nachiyar, Rani Gaidinliu, and Rani Chennamma have taken to new heights the role of women's power in defending and building the nation.

From the Santhal revolution, Paika revolution to Kol revolution and Bhil revolution, all these revolutions had strengthened the tribal contribution in the freedom struggle. We derived inspiration from the sacrifice of 'Dharti Aaba' Bhagwan Birsa Munda Ji for social upliftment and patriotism. I am happy that many museums are being built across the country dedicated to the role of the tribal communities in our freedom struggle.

Ladies and Gentlemen,

In 75 years as a parliamentary democracy, India has carried forward the resolve of progress through participation and consensus. In our country full of diversities, we are engaged in the making of 'Ek Bharat - Shreshtha Bharat' by adopting many languages, religions, sects, food habits, lifestyles and customs. This Amritkaal, which commences with the 75th year of our independence, is a period of new resolutions for India.

Today I see my country inspired and ready to welcome this new era with new thinking. Today India is adding a new chapter of development in every field.

The kind of capability that India has shown in combating the global crisis of Corona pandemic has enhanced India's credibility all over the world. We Indians not only faced this global challenge with our efforts but also set new standards for the world.

Just a few days ago, India set a record of administering 200 crore doses of corona vaccine. The patience, courage, and cooperation shown by the people of India in this entire battle is a symbol of our growing strength and sensitivity as a society. India not only took care of itself in these difficult situations but also helped the world. In the atmosphere created by the Corona pandemic, today, the world is looking at India with a new confidence. The international community has high hopes from India for ensuring global economic stability, ease of supply chain, and peace. In the coming months, India is also going to host the G-20 Group under its chairmanship. In this grouping, twenty big countries of the world will brainstorm on global issues under the chairmanship of India.

I am sure that the conclusions and policies that will emerge from this brainstorming in India will determine the direction of the coming decades.

Ladies and Gentlemen,

Decades ago, I had the opportunity to work as a teacher at Sri Aurobindo Integral School in Rairangpur. After a few days, we will observe the 150th birth anniversary of Sri Aurobindo. Sri Aurobindo's thoughts on education continue to inspire me. I have had an active association with educational institutions, serving in various positions as a public representative and then as a governor.

I have closely observed the enthusiasm and self-confidence of the youth of the country. Our revered Atal ji used to say that when the youth of the country progress, they not only create their own destiny but also shape the fate of the country. Today we are witnessing it come true.

Moving ahead in every field - from 'Vocal for Local' to 'Digital India' - today's India, marching in step with the world, is all set for 'Industrial Revolution Four Point O'. The youth of India have a big role in creating a record number of start-ups, in numerous innovations and in the adoption of digital technology in far flung areas. In the past few years, a new energy has been infused in the country due to the decisions taken and policies formulated for women empowerment.

I want all our sisters and daughters to be empowered more and more so that they continue to increase their contribution in every field of nation building.

I want to tell the youth of our country that you are not only building your own future but also laying the foundation of the India of the future. As the President of the country, I will always extend my full cooperation to you.

Ladies and Gentlemen,

Growth and progress mean continuously marching ahead, but equally important is awareness about one's past. Today, when the world is talking about a sustainable planet, the role of India's ancient traditions and sustainable lifestyle becomes more important. I was born in that tribal tradition which has lived in harmony with nature for thousands of years. I have realized the importance of forests and water bodies in my life. We take necessary resources from nature and serve nature with equal reverence. This sensitivity has become a global imperative today. I am happy that India is guiding the world in the field of environmental protection.

Ladies and Gentlemen,

In my life so far, I have realised the meaning of life only through public service.

There is a line from the poem of Bhim Bhoi Ji, a famous poet of Shri Jagannath Kshetra-

"Mo Jeeban pachhe narke padi thau, jagato uddhar heu".

That is, working for the welfare of the world is far greater than one's own interests.With this spirit of welfare of the world, I will always be ready to work with full devotion and dedication to live up to the trust you all have reposed in me.

Let us all unite and move forward on the path of duty with a dedicated spirit to build a glorious and self-reliant India.

Thank you, Jai Hind!

(Here is the English translation of her speech. The translation is provided by the concerned department and is gratefully acknowledged.)

https://presidentofindia.nic.in/writereaddata/Portal/Speech/Document/945/2_sph250722.pdf

https://presidentofindia.nic.in/speeches-detail.htm?945

President Droupadi Murmu's Oath Ceremony & Other pics

Her family pic

Droupadi Murmu's house at her village

She sweeps temple floor at her village

With her daughter & grandson

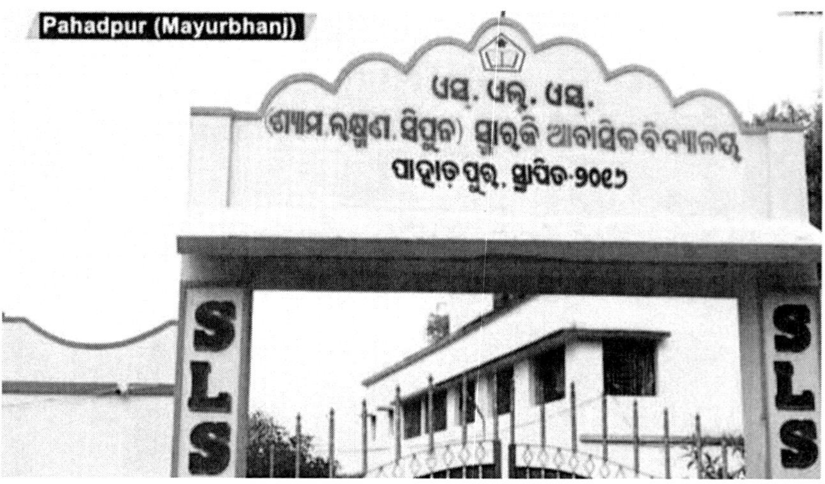

Her school at Mayurbhanj (Odisha)

She takes oath as the 15th President of India

Her first speech after taking oath

PM Modi Greets Her

President Droupadi Murmu being greeted by
former president Ram Nath Kovind